The Christmas
Revels songbook

DATE			

© THE BAKER & TAYLOR CO.

THE CHRISTMAS REVELS SONGBOOK

THE
CHRISTMAS REVELS
SONGBOOK

IN CELEBRATION
OF THE WINTER SOLSTICE

Carols, Processionals, Rounds, Ritual and Children's Songs

COMPILED BY NANCY & JOHN LANGSTAFF
FOREWORD BY SUSAN COOPER

David R. Godine ✦ Publisher ✦ Boston

First edition published in 1985 by David R. Godine, Publisher, Inc.
306 Dartmouth Street, Boston, Massachusetts 02116

Copyright © 1985 by John and Nancy Langstaff

Library of Congress Cataloging-in-Publication Data

Main entry under title:
The Christmas Revels songbook.
   1. Carols, English. 2. Christmas music.
I. Langstaff, John M. II. Langstaff, Nancy.
III. Cooper, Susan. IV. Revels, Inc.
M1495.C5586 1985   85-70140
    ISBN 0-87923-591-8 (flexi)

First edition

Printed in the United States of America

TABLE OF CONTENTS

Foreword vii
Introduction. ix

A FEAST OF SONGS

Alle Psallite cum Luya. 2
Brightest and Best 4
The Truth from Above 7
Bells in the High Tower. 8
Christmas Eve is Here. 10
Deck the Hall 12
Go, Tell It on the Mountain 14
Huron Indian Carol 16
Green Grow'th the Holly. 19
Jolly Old Hawk. 20
Mary Had a Baby. 24
Milford 26
King Herod and the Cock 29
O Little Town of Bethlehem 30
On Christmas Night 32
Silent Night 34
Star in the East 36
The Cherry Tree Carol 38
The Christ Child's Lullaby 40
The First Nowell. 42
The Truth Sent from Above 45
The Lord of the Dance 46
The Moon Shines Bright 49
The Twelve Days of Christmas 50
While Shepherds Watch'd Their Flocks . 55
Wondrous Love. 58

PROCESSIONALS

Exultation 62
I Saw Three Ships 64
Masters in This Hall. 66
Orientis Partibus. 73
Personent Hodie (On This Day). 74
Nova! Nova! 79
Sing We Noël. 80

Wexford Carol. 83
The Babe of Bethlehem 86

RITUAL SONGS

Apple Tree Wassail. 90
Abbots Bromley Horn Dance Tune. . . . 93
Cornish Wassail 94
Gloucestershire Wassail 96
Gower Wassail. 98
Please to See the King. 103
Kentucky Wassail 104
Somerset Wassail 106
The Holly and the Ivy. 109
Sussex Mummers' Carol 112
The Boar's Head Carol 114

CHILDREN'S SONGS

As I Sat on a Sunny Bank 118
Children, Go Where I Send Thee 120
Dame, Get Up and Bake Your Pies . . . 123
The Carol of the Birds 124
The Friendly Beasts. 126
The Wren Song. 128
There Was a Pig Went Out to Dig. 130
We've Been Awhile A-wandering 132
What Shall I Give to the Child?. 134
Glory to the Mountain 137
Here We Come A-wassailing 138

ROUNDS

A Christmas Round 142
Oken Leaves 143
Dona Nobis Pacem. 143
Peace Round 144
Shalom Chaverim 144
The Alleluia Round 145

Index of Titles. 146
Index of First Lines 147

FOREWORD

FOR HUNDREDS OF FAMILIES in Boston, Cambridge, New York and Washington, D. C., "Christmas wouldn't be Christmas without the Revels." They crowd into the theaters where local companies annually present John Langstaff's unique program of celebration, *The Christmas Revels;* they watch and wonder, and rejoice in the season. And above all, they happily obey the exhortation of a familiar bright-robed figure on the stage: *"Sing!"*

John Langstaff has been making people sing for more than thirty years; transmitting his enthusiasm in theaters, schools, universities and concert-halls, through radio and television — even through the mute printed page. In this new collection of songs, compiled with the collaboration of his wife, Nancy, he brings together for the first time much of the music with which *Christmas Revels* programs celebrate the turning of the year. For anyone who has ever experienced a Revels, this book is a lovely bulging Christmas stocking of familiar music; for everyone else, it's a joyful voyage of discovery through one of the best and most unusual collections of seasonal songs and carols ever made.

Read on — and sing!

SUSAN COOPER

ACKNOWLEDGMENTS

We acknowledge permission to use copyright material granted by Oxford University Press for "Forest Green," collected and arranged by Ralph Vaughan Williams, from the *English Hymnal;* by Penguin Books Ltd. for "The Boar's Head Carol" from *The Penguin Book of Christmas Carols,* ed. Elizabeth Poston © Elizabeth Poston 1965; by Galaxy Music Corporation, N.Y. for "Lord of the Dance" from *Sydney Carter: In the Present Tense* © 1963 by Galliard, Ltd. All Rights Reserved; by G. Schirmer, Inc. for John Jacob Niles's "The Kentucky Wassail" and "The Carol of the Birds" © 1943.

Other copyrights are held by composers/arrangers Marshall Barron, John Edmunds, Jerome Epstein, Brian Holmes and Marlene Montgomery. "The Holly and the Ivy" is from the estate of Maud Karpeles, administered by Peter Kennedy, Bristol, England.

The woodcuts reproduced on pp. 14, 15, 55, 74, and 114 are by Fritz Kredel. The illustration "Bethlehem" from *A Book of Christmas Carols,* selected and illustrated by Haig and Regina Shekerjian, copyright © 1963, 1977 by Haig and Regina Shekerjian, is reprinted by permission of Harper & Row, Publishers, Inc.

Christmas Revels is a registered service mark of Revels, Inc., all rights reserved. It is used here by permission.

Twenty-four of these songs have been recorded on *The Christmas Revels Record* (CR 1078) and *Wassail! Wassail!* (CR 1082), released by Revels Records, Box 502, Cambridge, Massachusetts 02139.

INTRODUCTION

THIS BOOK may well have started with our families' carol parties sixty years ago. My mother and father began inviting friends in to sing carols on the Sunday night before Christmas, the year I was born. But I was soon a small part of their musical party: hearing my father sing the ballad of "King Herod and the Cock" accompanied by my mother at the piano; miming the Page to his King Wenceslas as everyone sang the chorus; struggling to remember to sing out at the right moment as the verses of "The Twelve Days of Christmas" were divided among our family; and singing "The Friendly Beasts" with my brothers and sister. The guests, crowded into the candlelit house on Brooklyn Heights, joined in singing the well-known carols and our favorite Bach chorales and rounds. The spicy smell of hot wassail brewing on the stove all day permeated the house.

Nancy's musical family held their Christmas party about the same time in Manhattan, with Nancy and her mother at the two pianos, her father at his 'cello, and her sister, Marshall, playing violin.

The carolling "waits" met on Christmas Eve, my birthday, at our house. My parents would lead the singers out into the streets and from house to house through the Heights, gathering more and more neighbors to sing as the night progressed. Later, as a choir boy for six years at Grace Church in New York, I took part in the candlelight processionals and beautiful Christmas music we sang at the carol services. And later still, I taught many secular carols and ritual songs to the children at the Potomac School, Washington, D.C., and at Shady Hill School, Cambridge, and added dance and drama to the music in their Christmas plays and assemblies.

When I conceived the idea of a Revels production, I drew on many of these experiences to design a celebratory form of theater which incorporated traditional music, drama, dance and ritual—with an emphasis on audience participation. Thousands of Revels-goers have now sung many of our songs. It seems appropriate, therefore, to gather together a collection of these carols in a *Christmas Revels Songbook*, for friends to sing together, and for larger groups to use in celebrations at the Winter Solstice.

The Winter Solstice, that cold, dark time in December when the year turns again towards the coming of light, has been important since ancient times, long before Christianity and Judaism. We once lived our lives in close touch with the changing seasons, always wondering and fearful of what might or might not come to pass at the darkest time of year, hoping that our song, our mime, our dance could work as a propitiation to Nature, to ensure the return of Spring, warmth and new life. Many of our carols reflect these ancient concerns. The belief that the king must die for the survival of the community is found not only in the winter folk plays of the mummers, but also in a tradition like the hunting of the "king of all birds" on December 26. Our children in the Revels sing and mime an old mummers' carol about planting and harvesting, a survival of early agrarian magic-making. The children take over, as well, the old begging or collecting processionals that were once sung in the street, offering luck and abundance in exchange for a penny. In the wassail carols, one can imagine a singing group of street *waits* visiting a neighborhood to bring good luck to each household for the new year to come, and in turn to partake of a special wassail from a common bowl. There are even ritual aspects in the repetitive singing of accumulative carols: once upon a time we thought that the magic would work best if an incantation were repeated again and again.

Some of these carols, from oral tradition, are anonymous and timeless, with sources from the distant past; others go back to the Middle Ages, to the time of minstrels, ballads, mystery and miracle plays performed outside the Gothic cathedrals. Stemming from that mediæval period are two important characteristics of the carol: joyousness, which permeates much of the meaning and informs the interpretation; and the quality of dance, which derives from the original meaning of the *carol* (i.e., to take hands, singing and dancing in a ring). Certainly, many of our carols can be traced to danced songs, children's skipping games, and ritual processionals. The spirit of dance should always be integral to our music-making.

The processional was an important part of early ceremonies. And for those interested in producing Revels-like performances, processionals are wonderful ways to bring movement into song, to make a strong musical entrance, to have sound move about a hall, to incorporate colorful banners, to move people about an area, indoors or out. Not only can instruments be a part of a procession, but tumblers, jugglers, stilt walkers and even animals may be added for certain festive songs. Separated files of singers a distance apart can present problems in keeping together musically, but a good drum or tambourine beat will help sustain the pulse. Following the custom of the Middle Ages, it is effective to have the procession pause during the singing of a stanza, focusing attention on the solo or small group of singers, then resume travelling onward as the refrain or chorus part is sung.

Two exciting moments in the Christmas Revels have become "traditional" over the years: "The Lord of the Dance," which begins on the stage with singers and dancers, then reaches out into the audience of more than a thousand people who join hands in long lines to sing and dance out of the theater; and the "Sussex Mummers' Carol," which is always sung at the final curtain, with the audience joining the cast in singing with the brass and tympani.

Rounds or canons are a fine way to get a group of people to make music together—to sing in harmony. The rounds I have used in Christmas Revels productions (some of which are included in this collection) are simple enough for an audience to learn quickly, but are extraordinarily moving when more than a thousand voices divide into sections and realize the full harmonic sound. Some members of the audience may have never experienced this communal making of music before, and it suddenly seems magical to them as it all comes together.

We have included a few descants for singing or for playing on any appropriate instrument. (These are written at concert pitch, so that a transposition may be necessary for certain instruments.) If handbells are available, they make a splendid effect with certain carols, and can be rung even while processing. A guitar can be used as an alternative to the piano, to accompany the tune only. Suggestions for guitar chords are given; if the written key is difficult to manage, a capo bar is indicated to provide a familiar chord-shape for the same harmonic result. (The chord-shapes you would use with a capo are in parenthesis.)

We dedicate this volume to those singers who make this music come alive at Revels performances. Do join them in celebrating the season—and waken the earth with your singing!

J. L.

A FEAST OF SONGS

ALLE PSALLITE CUM LUYA

This mediæval motet can be performed with instruments doubling the melodic lines. Handbells and light percussion are also effective.

lively   ♩.=112   13th century French conductus

INTRODUCTORY
CHORD SUNG,
OR PLAYED ON
HANDBELLS
OR OTHER
INSTRUMENTS

3

BRIGHTEST AND BEST

A folk hymn, from the oral tradition of the Ritchie family of Kentucky, which is a variant of the early American shape-note hymn "Star in the East."

trad. Appalachian
arr. Jerome Epstein

legato ♩=69

SOLO

Hail the blest morn!_ See the Great Me-di-a-tor
Shep-herds, go wor-ship the Babe in the man-ger;

Down from the re-gions of Glo-ry de-scend!
Lo, for a guard_ the bright an-gels at-tend.

SOPRANO
ALTO I

Bright-est and best of the sons of the morn-ing!

ALTO II

Dawn on our dark - ness and lend us thine aid;

Star in the east, the hor - i - zon a - dorn - ing,

Guide where our In - fant Re - deem - er is laid.

5

2. Cold on His cradle the dew-drops are shining;
Low lies His bed, with the beasts of the stall;
Angels adore Him, in slumber reclining,
Wise men and shepherds before Him do fall.

Brightest and best of the sons of the morning!
Dawn on our darkness, and lend us Thine aid;
Star in the East, the horizon adorning,
Guide where our Infant Redeemer is laid.

3. Shall we not yield Him, in costly devotion,
Odours of Eden, and offerings divine,
Gems from the mountain, and pearls from the ocean,
Myrrh from the forest, and gold from the mine.

Brightest and best . . . &c.

THE TRUTH FROM ABOVE

This Dorian tune is a good example of the connection one can sometimes hear between folksong and plainsong. It is effective without any accompaniment—the way Ralph Vaughan Williams first heard it sung at King's Pyon, Herefordshire.

sustained ♩ = 138   trad. English

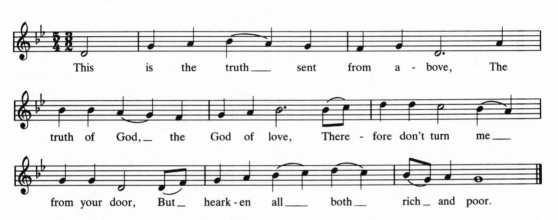

This is the truth___ sent from a - bove, The truth of God,___ the God of love, There - fore don't turn me___ from your door, But__ heark - en all___ both__ rich__ and poor.

2. And at that season of the year
Our blest Redeemer did appear;
He here did live, and here did preach,
And many thousands He did teach.

BELLS IN THE HIGH TOWER

Long, legato singing lines are called for. A solo verse could be sung, or a "bell verse" played, with the four parts hummed as accompaniment.

trad. Hungarian
arr. Marlene Montgomery

quietly ♩=69

*Bells needed: D E F G A B C d e

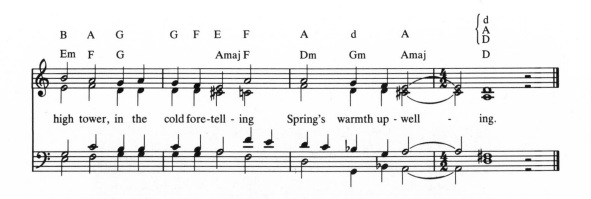

high tower, in the cold fore-tell - ing   Spring's warmth up - well   -   ing.

2. Bells in the cold tower, 'midst the snow of winter
Sound out the Spring song, that we may remember
Bells in the cold tower, after the long snowing
Come months of growing.

CHRISTMAS EVE IS HERE

Sung in a free chant-like fashion, this quiet carol sounds well with handbells.

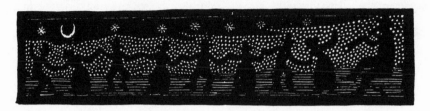

early French carol
arr. Marshall Barron

smoothly and freely ♩=76

BELLS*:

Christ-mas Eve is here, See the moon is wak-ing!

GUITAR:

Christ-mas Eve is here, Clear and cold the night. Trudg-ing through the snow,

*Bells needed: C D E G A

10

Go the qui - et peo - ple; Trudg - ing through the snow,
Go the qui - et peo - ple, Christ-mas Eve is here, Clear and cold the night.

2. People on the road
Carry lighted lanterns;
See their bobbing lights
Lead the way to church.
There they will keep watch
Till the hour of midnight,
There they will keep watch
Till the hour of midnight,
When the bells will ring
Joyous melodies.

3. Hear the ringing bells
Swinging far their music,
Hear the ringing bells
Playing merry chimes!
Christmas day is here,
Day of joy and gladness,
Christmas day is here,
Day of joy and gladness,
Bringing peace on earth,
And good will to men.

DECK THE HALL

A New Year's Eve carol, "Nos Galen."

Welsh

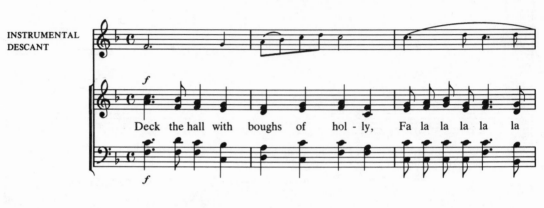

Deck the hall with boughs of hol - ly, Fa la la la la   la

la   la   la.   'Tis   the sea - son   to   be   jol - ly,

Fa   la   la   la   la   la   la   la   la.   Don   we   now   our

gay ap-par - el; Fa la la la la la la la la. Troll the an-cient

Yule - tide car - ol, Fa la la la la_____ la la la la.

la la

2. See the blazing Yule before us,
   Fa la la la la la la la la.
Strike the harp and join the chorus,
   Fa la la . . . &c.
Follow me in merry measure,
   Fa la la . . . &c.
While I tell of Yuletide treasure,
   Fa la la . . . &c.

3. Fast away the old year passes,
   Fa la la . . . &c.
Hail the new, ye lads and lasses,
   Fa la la . . . &c.
Sing we joyous all together,
   Fa la la . . . &c.
Heedless of the wind and weather,
   Fa la la . . . &c.

13

GO, TELL IT ON THE MOUNTAIN!

This spiritual can be exciting, bursting forth in juxtaposition with a reading from *St. Luke*, Chapter II.

Black American
arr. Marshall Barron

exultantly ♩=84

Go, tell it on the moun-tain, O-ver the hills and ev-'ry-where!

Go, tell it on the moun-tain That Je-sus Christ is born! While

Fine VERSE

Fine

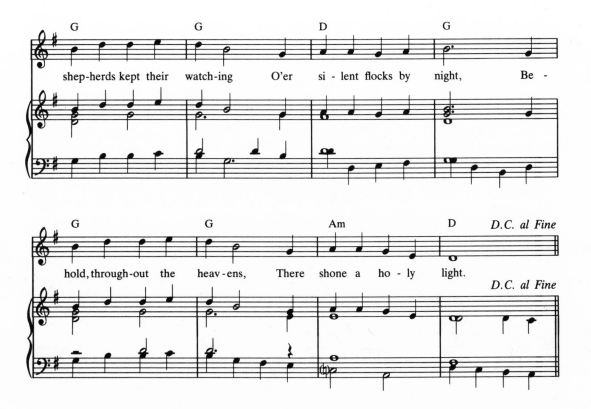

shep-herds kept their watch-ing O'er si - lent flocks by night, Be -

hold, through-out the heav-ens, There shone a ho - ly light.

D.C. al Fine

2. The shepherds feared and trembled,
When lo! above the earth
Rang out the angel chorus
That hailed our Jesus' birth.

> *Go, tell it on the mountain,*
> *Over the hills and ev'rywhere!*
> *Go, tell it on the mountain*
> *That Jesus Christ is born!*

3. And lo! when they had heard it
They all bowed down and prayed;
Then travelled on together
To where the Babe was laid.

> *Go, tell it . . . &c.*

4. Down in a lowly manger,
The humble Babe was born;
And God sent down His angels
That blessed Christmas morn.

> *Go, tell it . . . &c.*

HURON INDIAN CAROL

Although this carol is not representative of indigenous Native American music, it is an instance of one culture absorbing and reshaping the elements of another. Taught by Jesuit missionaries, the Huron Indians made Jesus the son of Gitchi-manitou. He was wrapped in swaddling clothes of rabbit skins, laid within a birchbark teepee, and worshipped by hunters and chiefs.

trad. American
arr. Marshall Barron

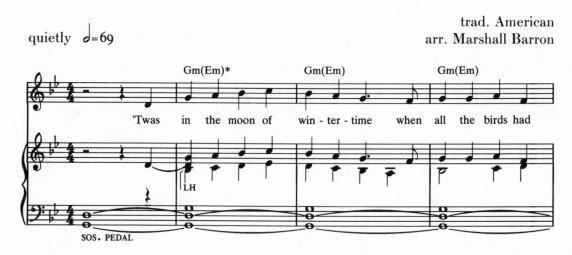

'Twas in the moon of win-ter-time when all the birds had

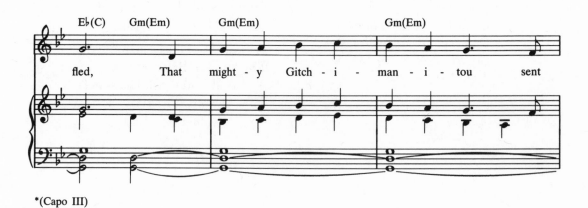

fled, That might-y Gitch-i-man-i-tou sent

*(Capo III)

16

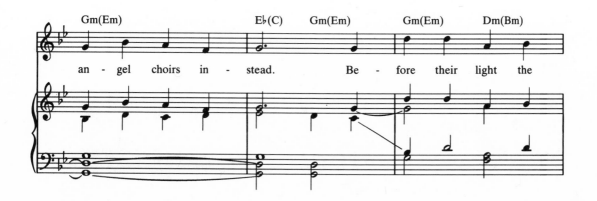

an - gel choirs in - stead. Be - fore their light the

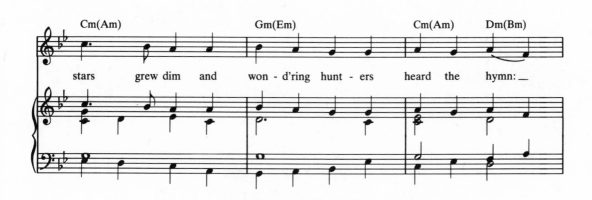

stars grew dim and won - d'ring hunt - ers heard the hymn: __

Je - sus, your King is born, Je - sus is

17

born, in ex - cel - sis glo - ri - a.

2. Within a lodge of broken bark
The tender Babe was found,
A ragged robe of rabbit skin
Enwrapped His beauty round.
The chiefs from far before Him knelt
With gifts of fox and beaver pelt.

Jesus, your King is born,
Jesus is born,
In excelsis gloria.

3. O children of the forest free,
O sons of Manitou,
The Holy Child of earth and heav'n
Is born today for you.
Come kneel before the radiant Boy
Who brings you beauty, peace and joy.

Jesus, your King is born . . . &c.

GREEN GROW'TH THE HOLLY

This three-part song is attributed to King Henry VIII.

16th century mss.
British Museum

 = 104

SOPRANO
ALTO

Green grow'th the hol - ly, So doth the i - vy; Though win - ter

TENOR

Green grow'th the hol - ly,___ So doth the i - vy; Though win - ter

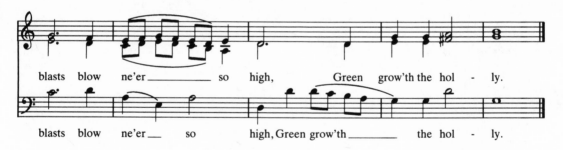

blasts blow ne'er_____ so high, Green grow'th the hol - ly.

blasts blow ne'er__ so high, Green grow'th_____ the hol - ly.

2. Green grow'th the holly
So doth the ivy;
The God of life can never die,
Hope! saith the holly.

JOLLY OLD HAWK

"Jolly Old Hawk" is an unusual variant of "The Twelve Days of Christmas," as sung by the Waterson family of Yorkshire. At a pub gathering, this forfeit song could be a test of one's quickness and memory — a mistake might cost the singer a round of beer!

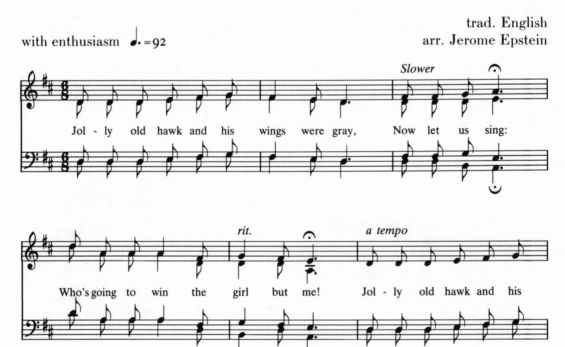

trad. English
arr. Jerome Epstein

with enthusiasm ♩.=92

Slower

Jol - ly old hawk and his wings were gray, Now let us sing:

rit.   a tempo

Who's going to win the girl but me! Jol - ly old hawk and his

20

wings were gray, Sent to my love on the twelfth most day: Twelve old

bears and they was a - roar - in', E-le - ven old mares_ and they was a -

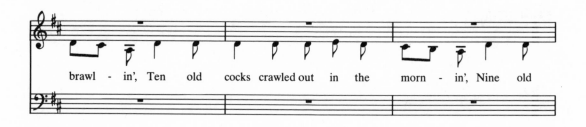

brawl - in', Ten old cocks crawled out in the morn - in', Nine old

CHORUS

boars_ and they was a - quar-rel - in', Jol - ly old hawk and his wings were

gray, Sent to my love on the twelfth most day: Eight old bulls and

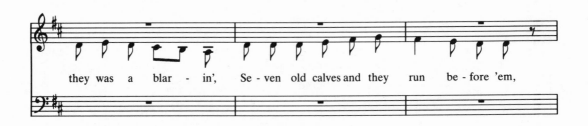

they was a blar - in', Se - ven old calves and they run be - fore 'em,

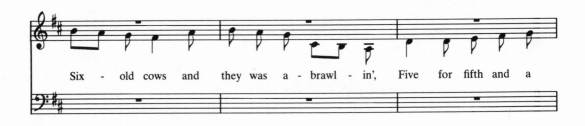

Six - old cows and they was a - brawl - in', Five for fifth and a

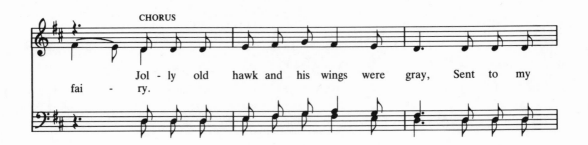

fai - ry. Jol - ly old hawk and his wings were gray, Sent to my

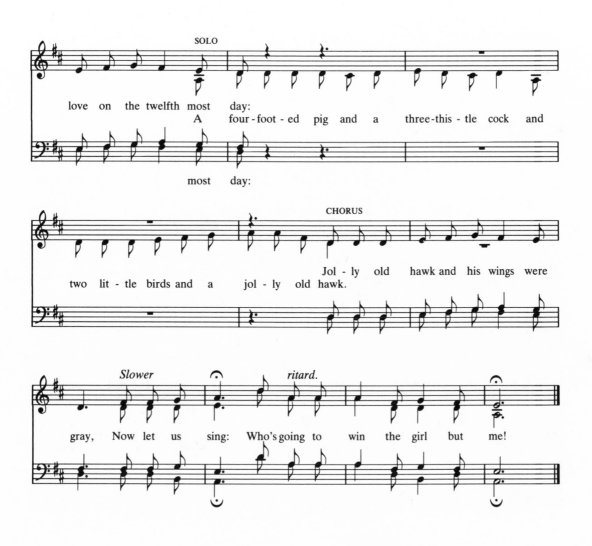

love on the twelfth most day: A four - foot - ed pig and a three - this - tle cock and

most day:

two lit - tle birds and a jol - ly old hawk.

Jol - ly old hawk and his wings were

Slower ⌢ *ritard.*

gray, Now let us sing: Who's going to win the girl but me!

MARY HAD A BABY

This carol is an example of simple storytelling in which the leader can improvise in "lining out" each verse for the group to follow.

Black American tradition
arr. Marshall Barron

quietly and rhythmically ♩.=66

SOLO

Mar - y had a ba - by, oh, Lord, Mar - y had a ba - by,

oh, Lord, Mar - y had a ba - by, Mar - y had a ba - by,

24

Mar - y had a ba - by, *oh, Lord.*

2. Where did she lay Him? *oh, Lord,*
Where did she lay Him? *oh, Lord,*
Where did she lay Him?
Where did she lay Him?
Where did she lay Him? *oh, Lord.*

3. Laid Him in a manger, *oh, Lord* . . . &c.

4. What did she name Him? *oh, Lord* . . . &c.

5. Named Him King Jesus, *oh, Lord* . . . &c.

6. Who heard the singing? *oh, Lord* . . . &c.

7. Shepherds heard the singing, *oh, Lord* . . . &c.

8. Star kept a-shining, *oh, Lord* . . . &c.

MILFORD

Here is an example of an early American *fuguing tune*. Its fervor and harmonic sonority are enhanced by having some sopranos sing the melody line with the tenors, and adding some tenors to the soprano line on top. This sounds best unaccompanied.

John Stepheson, 1802
Sacred Harp hymnal

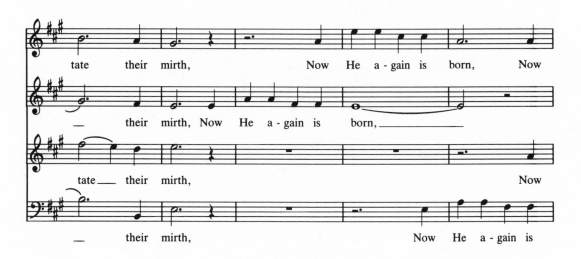

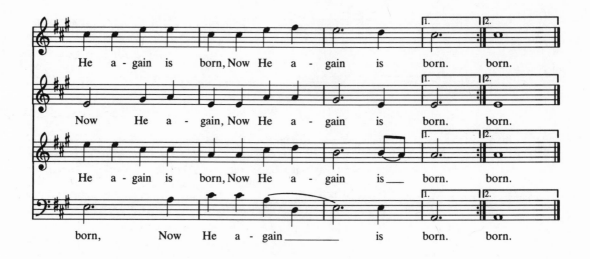

He a - gain is born, Now He a - gain is born. born.

Now He a - gain, Now He a - gain is born. born.

He a - gain is born, Now He a - gain is born. born.

born, Now He a - gain is born. born.

2. While shepherds watch'd their flocks by night,
While shepherds watch'd their flocks by night,
All seated on the ground;
The angel of the Lord came down,
And glory shone around,
And glory shone around,
And glory shone around.

3. All glory be to God on high,
All glory be to God on high,
And to the earth be peace.
Goodwill henceforth from heav'n to all,
Begin and never cease . . . &c.

KING HEROD AND THE COCK

This legendary ballad of a miraculous happening at the table of Herod has been traced to early Danish sources of 1200 A.D. The English variant was collected by Cecil Sharp in Worcestershire. The singing of the story should be straight-forward.

trad. English
arr. Jerome Epstein

♩=58

There was a star in Da-vid's land, In Da-vid's land ap-

peared; And in King Her-od's cham-ber So bright it did shine there.

2. The Wise Men they soon spied it,
And told the King a-nigh
That a Princely Babe was born that night,
No King shall e'er destroy.

3. "If this be the truth," King Herod said,
"That thou hast told to me,
The roasted cock that lies in the dish
Shall crow full senses three."

4. O the cock soon thrustened and feathered well,
By the work of God's own hand,
And he did crow full senses three
In the dish where he did stand!

29

O LITTLE TOWN OF BETHLEHEM
(Forest Green)

The words of this Christmas hymn were written by Bishop Phillips Brooks after he had visited Bethlehem in 1866. Vaughan Williams set the text to the folk tune "The Ploughboy's Dream," which he had collected at Forest Green, Surrey, in 1903.

trad. English tune
arr. Ralph Vaughan Williams

O lit-tle town of Beth-le-hem, How still we see thee lie! A-bove thy deep and dream-less sleep The si-lent stars go

by; Yet_ in thy dark_ streets_ shin - eth The ev - er - last - ing

Light; The hopes and fears of all _ the _ years Are met in _ thee to - night.

2. For Christ is born of Mary,
And gathered all above,
While mortals sleep, the angels keep
Their watch of wondering love.
O morning stars, together
Proclaim the holy birth!
And praises sing to God the King,
And peace to men on earth.

3. How silently, how silently
The wondrous gift is given!
So God imparts to human hearts
The blessings of His heaven.
No ear may hear His coming,
But in this world of sin,
Where meek souls will receive Him, still
The dear Christ enters in.

4. O holy Child of Bethlehem!
Descend to us, we pray;
Cast out our sin and enter in,
Be born in us today.
We hear the Christmas angels
The great glad tidings tell;
O come to us, abide with us,
Our Lord Emmanuel!

ON CHRISTMAS NIGHT

This folk carol was collected by Ralph Vaughan Williams at Monk's Gate, Sussex, in 1904. Its first phrase can be sung antiphonally with a divided chorus. The carol's dancelike quality lends itself well to choreography.

lightly ♩.=92

trad. English
arr. Marshall Barron

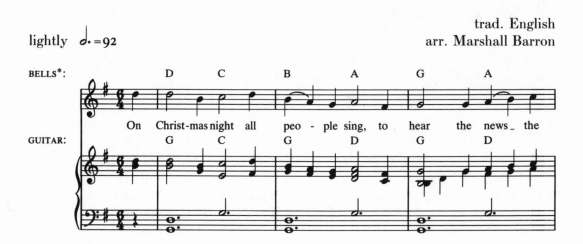

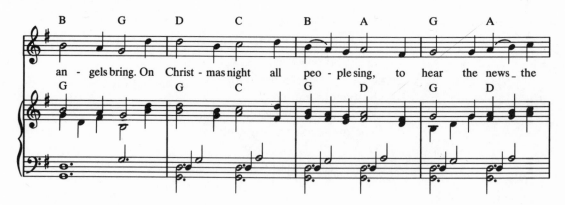

*Bells needed: G A B C D E

an - gels bring; News of great joy,— news of—— great

mirth,—— News of our mer - ci - ful— King's birth.——

2. When sin departs before Thy grace,
Then life and health come in its place;
When sin departs before Thy grace,
Then life and health come in its place;
Angels and men with joy may sing,
All for to see the newborn King.

3. All out of darkness we have light,
Which made the angels sing this night;
All out of darkness we have light,
Which made the angels sing this night;
'Glory to God and peace to men,
Now and for evermore. Amen.'

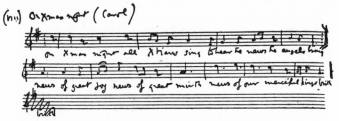

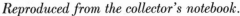

Reproduced from the collector's notebook.

33

SILENT NIGHT

The first time "Stille Nacht" was heard, it was accompanied on guitar, as the organ in the village church was broken.

quietly ♩.=42

Franz Gruber
descant Channing Lefebvre

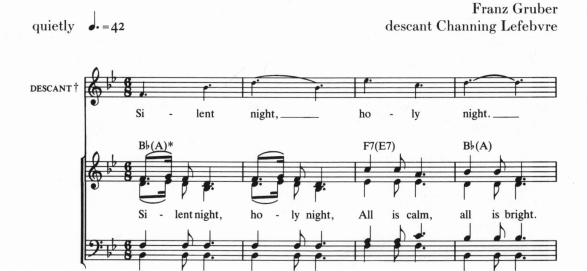

DESCANT †

Si - lent night, _____ ho - ly night. _____

Bb(A)*   F7(E7)   Bb(A)

Si - lent night, ho - ly night, All is calm, all is bright.

*(Capo I)
†Descant sung to second verse;
third verse instruments only.

34

Glo - ries stream from heav'n a - - far. _____

E♭(D) B♭(A) E♭(D) B♭(A)

'Round yon Vir - gin Moth - er and Child. Ho - ly In - fant so tend - er and mild,

Al - le - - lu - ia, Christ is born! ___

F7(E7) B♭(A) F7(E7) B♭(A)

Sleep in hea - ven - ly peace, ___ Sleep _ in hea - ven - ly peace. ___

2. Silent night, holy night,
Shepherds quake at the sight,
Glories stream from heaven afar,
Heav'nly hosts sing Alleluia;
Christ, the Saviour, is born,
Christ, the Saviour, is born!

3. Silent night, holy night,
Son of God, love's pure light
Radiant beams from Thy holy face,
With the dawn of redeeming grace,
Jesus, Lord, at Thy birth,
Jesus, Lord, at Thy birth.

STAR IN THE EAST

The traditional tune for "Brightest and Best" has an obvious connection to this nineteenth-century four-part hymn, which illustrates how folk tunes often found their way into congregational singing.

shape-note hymn
from *Southern Harmony*, 1835
alto part Jerome Epstein

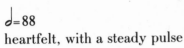

heartfelt, with a steady pulse

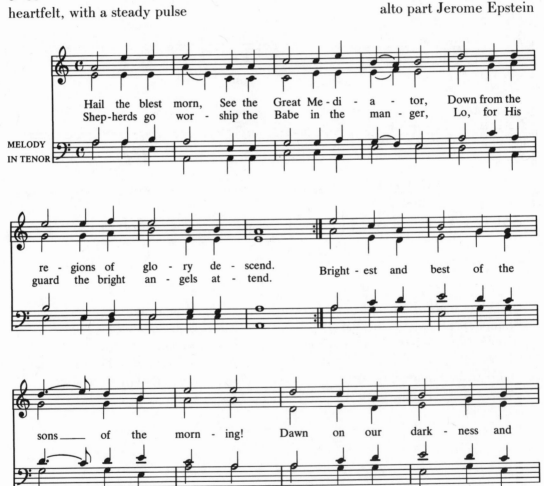

MELODY
IN TENOR

Hail the blest morn, See the Great Me - di - a - tor, Down from the
Shep-herds go wor - ship the Babe in the man - ger, Lo, for His

re - gions of glo - ry de - scend.
guard the bright an - gels at - tend.

Bright - est and best of the

sons of the morn - ing! Dawn on our dark - ness and

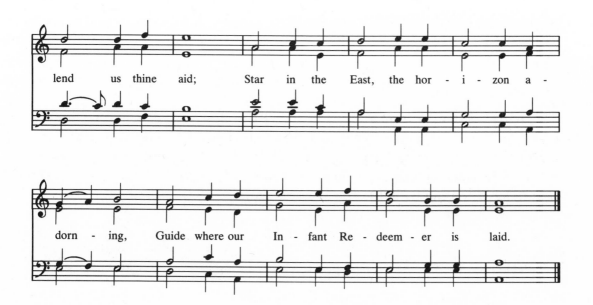

lend   us   thine   aid;   Star   in   the   East,   the   hor - i - zon   a -

dorn - ing,   Guide   where our   In - fant   Re - deem - er   is   laid.

2. Cold on His cradle the dew-drops are shining;
Low lies His bed, with the beasts of the stall;
Angels adore Him, in slumbers reclining,
Wise men and shepherds before Him do fall.

> *Brightest and best of the sons of the morning!*
> *Dawn on our darkness, and lend us Thine aid;*
> *Star in the East, the horizon adorning,*
> *Guide where our Infant Redeemer was laid.*

3. Say, shall we yield Him, in costly devotion,
Odours of Eden, and offerings divine,
Gems from the mountain, and pearls from the ocean,
Myrrh from the forest, and gold from the mine.

> *Brightest and best . . . &c.*

THE CHERRY TREE CAROL

This narrative ballad from Kentucky shows the close connection between the ballad and the carol, both of which had their greatest popularity in the fifteenth century. Sources for this legendary carol go back to a fifth-century apochryphal gospel describing a palm tree. This later became an apple or cherry tree as oral tradition carried the ballad to the Western world.

trad. American
arr. Marshall Barron

moving gently ♩=76

When Jo-seph was an old man, an old man was he, He

court - ed Vir-gin Ma-ry the Queen of Gal-i-lee, He

*(Capo V)

38

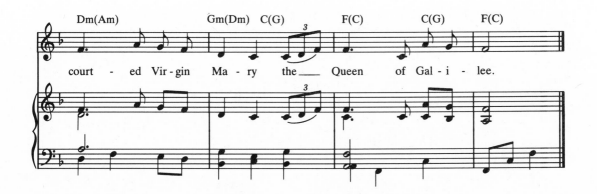

court - ed Vir - gin Ma - ry the Queen of Gal - i - lee.

2. As Joseph and Mary
Were walking one day,
"Here are apples, here are cherries
Enough to behold,
Here are apples, here are cherries
Enough to behold."

3. Then Mary spoke to Joseph,
So meek and so mild:
"Joseph, gather me some cherries,
For I am with child . . . &c."

4. Then Joseph flew in anger,
In anger flew he.
"Let the father of the baby
Gather cherries for thee . . . &c."

5. Then Jesus spoke a few words,
A few words spoke he:
"Let my mother have some cherries,
Bow low down, cherry tree . . . &c."

6. The cherry tree bowed low down,
Bowed low down to the ground,
And Mary gathered cherries
While Joseph stood around . . . &c.

7. Then Joseph took Mary
All on his right knee.
"What have I done, Lord?
Have mercy on me . . . &c."

8. Then Joseph took Mary
All on his left knee.
"Now tell me, little baby,
When thy birthday will be . . . &c."

9. "On the sixth day of January
My birthday will be,
When the stars and the elements
Shall tremble with glee! . . . &c"

THE CHRIST CHILD'S LULLABY
(Taladh Chriosta)

This song was collected by Marjory Kennedy-Fraser on the isle of Eriskay, and translated from the Gælic by Seamus Ennis.

trad. Hebridean
arr. Marshall Barron

smoothly ♩.= 50

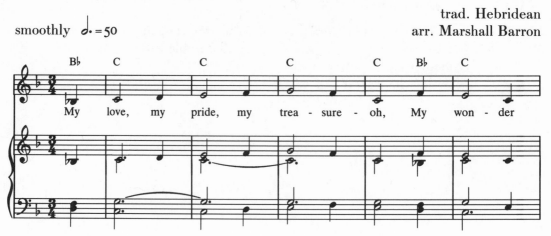

My love, my pride, my trea - sure - oh, My won - der

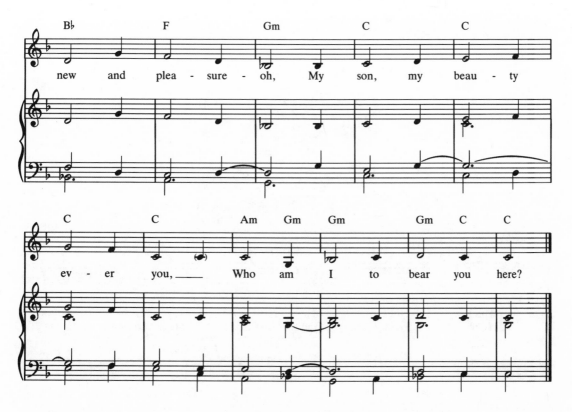

new and plea - sure - oh, My son, my beau - ty

ev - er you, ___ Who am I to bear you here?

For some verses, try the accompaniment an octave higher, while voice sings at original pitch.

2. The cause of talk and tale am I,
The cause of greatest fame am I,
The cause of proudest care on high
To have for mine the King of all.

3. And though you are the King of all,
They sent you to the manger stall,
When at your feet they all should fall
And glorify my child the King.

4. There shone a star above three kings
To guide them to the King of Kings,
They held you in their humble arms
And knelt before you until dawn.

5. They gave you myrrh, they gave you gold,
Frankincense and gifts untold,
They travelled far these gifts to bring,
And kneel before their newborn King.

6. My love, my pride, my treasure—oh,
My wonder new and pleasure—oh,
My son, my beauty ever you,
Who am I to bear you here?

THE FIRST NOWELL

trad. English

The first Nowell the an-gel did say Was to cer-tain poor
They look-ed up and saw a Star Shin-ing in the

shep-herds in fields as they lay; In fields where they lay
East, be-yond them far, And to the earth it

keep-ing their sheep On a cold win-ter's night that was so deep.
gave great light, And so it con-tin-ued both day and night.

Now - ell, _ Now - ell, Now - ell, Now - ell, _ Born is the King _ of Is - ra - el.

DESCANT FOR VOICE OR INSTRUMENT

UNISON VOICES

This _ star _ drew _ nigh to _ the _ north - west O'er _ Beth - le -
And _ there _ it _ did both _ stop _ and stay Right _ o - ver the

hem _ it took _ its rest. Now - ell, _ Now - ell, Now -
place _ where Je - sus lay.

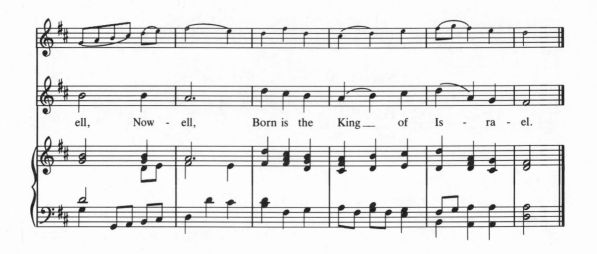

ell,   Now - ell,   Born is the   King __ of   Is - ra - el.

THE TRUTH SENT FROM ABOVE

Sing this carol unaccompanied as a street singer or town crier would through the village streets at dawn on Christmas Day. Cecil Sharp collected this variant from a singer in Donnington Wood, Shropshire.

smoothly ♩=48

trad. English

This is the truth sent from a - bove, The
truth of God, the God of love; There - fore don't turn me
from your door, But heark - en all, both rich and poor.

2. And at that season of the year
Our blest Redeemer did appear;
He here did live, and here did preach,
And many thousands He did teach.

3. God grant to all within this place
True saving faith—that special grace
Which to all people doth belong;
And thus I close my Christmas song.

45

THE LORD OF THE DANCE

This song, set to the Shaker tune "Simple Gifts," echos the imagery of the mediæval carol "Tomorrow Will Be My Dancing Day," whose final line reads "that man may come unto the general dance." In both, the energy of dance symbolizes a life-giving force.

words by Sydney Carter
arr. Jerome Epstein

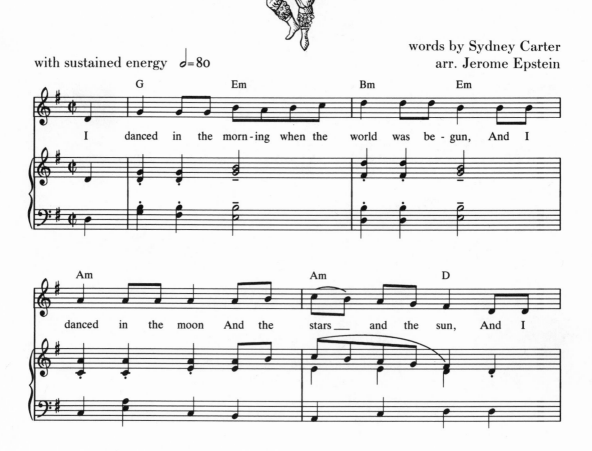

46

came down from hea - ven And I danced on the earth, At

Beth - le - hem I had my birth. Dance, then, where - ev - er you may be,

I am the Lord of the Dance, said he, And I'll lead you all, where -

ev - er you may be, And I'll lead you all in the Dance, said he.

2. "I danced for the scribe and the pharisee,
But they would not dance and they wouldn't follow me,
I danced for the fishermen, for James and John,
They came with me and the dance went on.

> *"Dance, then, wherever you may be,*
> *I am the Lord of the Dance," said he,*
> *"And I'll lead you all, wherever you may be,*
> *And I'll lead you all in the dance," said he.*

3. "I danced on the Sabbath and I cured the lame;
The holy people said it was a shame.
They whipped and they stripped and they hung me on high;
They left me there on a Cross to die.

> *"Dance, then, wherever you may be . . ."* &c.

4. "I danced on a Friday when the sky turned black;
It's hard to dance with the devil on your back;
They buried my body and they thought I'd gone;
But I am the dance and I still go on.

> *"Dance, then, wherever you may be . . ."* &c.

5. "They cut me down and I leapt up high;
I am the life that'll never, never die.
I'll live in you if you'll live in me;
I am the Lord of the Dance," said he.

> *"Dance, then, wherever you may be . . ."* &c.

48

THE MOON SHINES BRIGHT
(The Bellman's Song)

One can imagine hearing a lone singer's voice out in the village street. Cecil Sharp collected this carol in Warwickshire.

solemnly ♩=84

trad. English

The moon shines bright and the stars give a light A lit - tle be - fore it is day; Our Lord _ our _ God He call - ed _ on us And _ bids us a - wake _ and _ pray.

2. Awake! O awake, good people all,
Awake, and you shall hear:
Our Lord, our God was born on this day
For us whom He loved so dear.

3. My song it is done, and I must be gone,
No longer can I stay here.
God bless you all, both great and small,
And send you a happy New Year.

THE TWELVE DAYS OF CHRISTMAS

Although there are many variants of "The Twelve Days of Christmas," this version remains the most popular. Gifts are brought on each of the twelve days between Christmas and Twelfth Night. Custom has it that if you make a mistake in the singing, you pay a forfeit!

Partridge

trad. English
arr. Brian Holmes

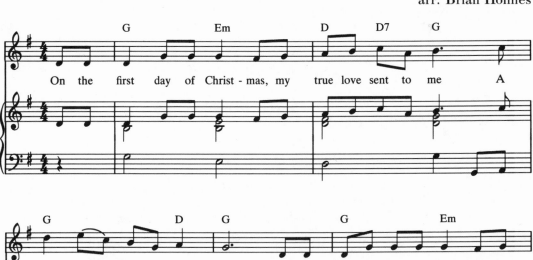

On the first day of Christ-mas, my true love sent to me A

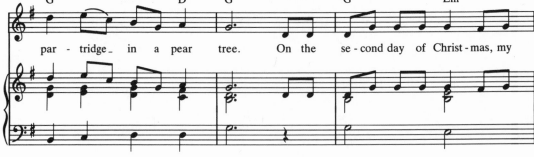

par - tridge in a pear tree. On the se - cond day of Christ-mas, my

true love sent to me   Two tur-tle doves, and a   par-tridge _ in a pear

tree.   On the   third day of Christ-mas My   true love sent to me

Three French _ hens,   Two tur-tle doves, And a   par-tridge _ in a pear

tree.   On the   fourth day of Christ-mas, my   true love sent to me,

On the sixth day of Christ-mas my true love sent to me / On the seventh. . . etc.

Six geese a-lay-ing, / Seven swans a-swim-ming, etc. Five gold rings, Four calling birds,

Three French hens, Two turtle doves, And a partridge in a pear tree.

al Segno

Fine

*cumulative measure repeated for subsequent "days" and "gifts."

8. On the eighth day of Christmas, my true love sent to me
    Eight maids a-milking . . . &c.

9. On the ninth day of Christmas, my true love sent to me
    Nine ladies dancing . . . &c.

10. On the tenth day of Christmas, my true love sent to me
     Ten lords a-leaping . . . &c.

11. On the eleventh day of Christmas, my true love sent to me
     Eleven pipers piping . . . &c.

12. On the twelfth day of Christmas, my true love sent to me
     Twelve drummers drumming . . . &c.

In Revels performances, this tune is often performed with Latin rhythms. Although the piano arrangement does not reflect this, the adventurous may use guitar instead, plus any percussion instruments at hand. The stress in the 4/4 measures should be:

for example: etc.

But in the 3/4 measures, the rhythm changes:

WHILE SHEPHERDS
WATCH'D THEIR FLOCKS

This favorite Christmas hymn, with words by the seventeenth-century Nahum Tate to an earlier tune, is often sung throughout the sheep country of Yorkshire and Lancastershire to the popular local tune "On Ilkla Moor Baht Hat."

trad. English
arr. Marshall Barron

with gusto ♩=92

While shep-herds watch'd their flocks by night   All seat-ed on the

flocks by night   all seat-ed on the

*(Capo III)

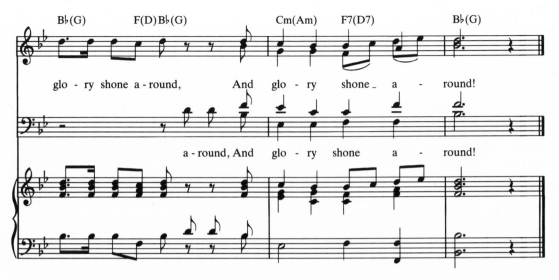

2. "Fear not," said he, for mighty dread (mighty dread)
     Had seized their troubled mind;
"Glad tidings of great joy I bring (Glad tidings of great joy I bring)
Glad tidings of great joy I bring (Glad tidings of great joy I bring)
     To you and all mankind (mankind),
     To you and all mankind (mankind),
     To you and all mankind."

3. "To you, in David's town this day (town this day)
     Is born of David's line, (David's line)
The Saviour, Who is Christ the Lord . . . &c.
     And this shall be the sign (the sign) . . . &c."

4. "The heavenly Babe you there shall find (there shall find)
     To human view displayed,
All meanly wrapped in swathing bands . . . &c.
     And in a manger laid (manger laid) . . . &c."

5. Thus spake the seraph, and forthwith (and forthwith)
     Appeared a shining throng
Of angels praising God, who thus . . . &c.
     Addressed their joyful song (joyful song) . . . &c."

6. "All glory be to God on high (God on high)
     And on the earth be peace;
Goodwill henceforth from heaven to men . . . &c.
Begin and never cease (never cease) . . . &c"

57

WONDROUS LOVE

This noble and moving hymn appears in many of the shape-note books, and variants of the tune are found in oral tradition. The early American device of doubling the octave is very effective here—have some of the sopranos join the tenors on the tune, and have a few tenors sing with the sopranos on their top line.

trad. American folk hymn
Sacred Harp, 1844

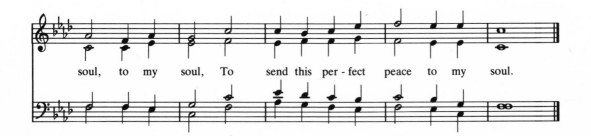

soul, to my soul, To send this per - fect peace to my soul.

2. Ye winged seraphs, fly! Bear the news, bear the news!
Ye winged seraphs, fly! Bear the news!
Ye winged seraphs fly like comets through the sky,
Fill vast eternity with the news, with the news,
Fill vast eternity with the news.

3. To God and to the Lamb, I will sing, I will sing!
To God and to the Lamb, I will sing!
To God and to the Lamb, who is the great I AM.
While millions join the theme, I will sing, I will sing,
While millions join the theme, I will sing.

PROCESSIONALS

EXULTATION

This tune, from the oral folk tradition, was included by William Walker in his hymnal of 1835.

with fervor ♩=108   *Southern Harmony* shape-note hymnal

*(Capo III)

2. Now with singing and praise, let us spend all our days
By our heavenly Father bestowed.
While His grace we receive from His bounty, and live
To the honor and glory of God.

3. There, oh! there at His feet, we shall all likewise meet,
And be parted in body no more;
We shall sing to our lyres with the heavenly choirs,
And our Saviour in glory adore.

Clapping on the offbeat would be effective.

I SAW THREE SHIPS

This popular carol, with its many variants, stems from apochryphal legends. The melody is a dance tune from the village of Helston in Cornwall. Taken at a brisk tempo, this carol can be sung and danced in the true spirit of the early *carole*.

trad. English
arr. Marshall Barron

lightly and rhythmically ♩=100

I saw three ships come sailing in, On Christ-mas Day, on Christ-mas Day, I saw three ships come sailing in, On Christ-mas Day in the morn - ing. And who was in those

ships all three, On __ Christ-mas Day, __ on __ Christ-mas Day? And

who was in those __ ships __ all __ three, On __ Christ-mas Day __ in the morn - ing?

2. 'Twas Joseph and his Fair Ladye,
      On Christmas Day, on Christmas Day.
'Twas Joseph and his Fair Ladye,
      On Christmas Day in the morning.

O, he did whistle and she did sing,
      On Christmas Day, on Christmas Day,
O, he did whistle and she did sing,
      On Christmas Day in the morning!

3. Saint Michael was the steeres-man,
      On Christmas Day . . . &c.
Saint Michael was . . . &c.
      On Christmas Day . . . &c.
Pray whither sailed those ships all three?
      On Christmas Day . . . &c.
Pray whither sailed . . . &c.

4. O, they sailed into Bethlehem,
      On Christmas Day . . . &c.
O, they sailed . . . &c.
      On Christmas Day . . . &c.

And all the bells on earth shall ring,
      On Christmas Day . . . &c.
And all the bells . . . &c.
      On Christmas Day . . . &c.

Any bells at hand can be shaken on the last lines of this carol, to add a joyous cacophony.

65

MASTERS IN THIS HALL

This mediæval tune from Chartres has words by William Morris.

majestically ♩.=88

arr. Jerome Epstein

BELLS*:
(first verse
only)

UNISON

1.Mas-ters in this hall, ___ Hear ye news to-
2. Go-ing o'er the hills, ___ Through the milk white

day, _____ Brought from o - ver sea, ___ And ev - er I you pray.
snow, _____ Heard I ew - es bleat _____ While the wind did blow.

*Bells needed: C D E F G A B♭ c d e

CHORUS *(verses 1-4)*

Now - ell, now - ell, now - ell, Now - ell sing we clear! Hol - pen

are all folk on earth, __ Born __ is God's son so dear,

Now - ell, now - ell, now - ell, Now - ell sing we loud! God to -

67

day hath poor folk raised _ And _ cast a-down the proud.

VERSE 3

S.

Then to Beth-lem town ___ We went two and two, ___ And

T.
B.

al Segno

in a sor - ry place ___ Heard the ox - en low.

VERSE 4

S.
A.

There - in did we _ see ___ A sweet _ and good - ly may ___

T.

68

al Segno

And a fair old man;____ Up - on__ the straw_ she lay.

VERSE 5

BELLS

S.
A.

This is Christ the Lord,____ Mas- _Mas- ters be ye glad!_____

T.

This is Christ the Lord,____ Mas - ters be ye glad!_____

BAR.
B.

Christ-mas is come in, _____ And no folk should _ be sad.

Christ-mas is come in, _____ And no folk should be sad.

CHORUS 5 (to last verse)

Now - ell, now - ell, now - ell Now - ell sing we clear! Hol - pen

Now - ell, now - ell, now - ell Now - ell sing we clear! Hol - pen

are all folk on earth, __ Born __ is God's son so dear __

are all folk on earth, __ Born is God's son so dear,

Now - ell, now - ell, now - ell Now - ell sing we loud! God to -

Now - ell, now - ell, now - ell, Now - ell sing we loud! God to -

day hath poor folk raised __ And __ cast a - down the proud.

day hath poor folk raised __ And cast a - down the proud.

ORIENTIS PARTIBUS

The "Song of the Ass," important in the early history of Western music, was sung during the Middle Ages as a processional at Sens, when a donkey was ridden into the Cathedral. The irrepressible popular humor of the Feast of Fools and similar mediæval festivals is found in the carol's "braying" refrain, which was sung by the clergy. (Compare this tune to the children's carol of "The Friendly Beasts.")

anon. mediæval carol
English words, Susan Cooper

simply

O - ri - en - tis par - ti - bus ad - ven - ta - vit a - si - nus,

pul - cher et for - tis - si - mus, Sar - ci - nis ap - tis - si - mus.

BELLS

Hez, Sir As - nes, hez!

1. From the East the donkey came,
Stout and strong as twenty men;
Ears like wings and eyes like flame,
Striding into Bethlehem.

Heh! Sir Ass, oh heh!

2. Faster than the deer he leapt,
With his burden on his back;
Though all other creatures slept,
Still the ass kept on his track.

Heh! Sir Ass, oh heh!

3. Still he draws his heavy load,
Fed on barley and rough hay;
Pulling on along the road—
Donkey, pull our sins away!

Heh! Sir Ass, oh heh!

4. Wrap him now in cloth of gold;
All rejoice who see him pass;
Mirth inhabit young and old
On this feast day of the ass.

Heh! Sir Ass, oh heh!

PERSONENT HODIE
(On This Day)

This carol is from the *Piæ Cantiones* in the British Museum. This historically famous collection of European songs was compiled by Theoderius Petrus in 1582.

14th century German
arr. Jerome Epstein
English words, J. M. Joseph

majestically ♩=76

*Bells needed: C D E F G A B c d e

Sum - mo De - o da - tus. _____ I - de - o - o - o, I - de -

o - o - o, I - de - o glo - ri - a in ex - cel - sis De - o.

On this day earth shall ring With the song chil - dren sing

To the Lord, to our King, Born on earth to save us;

Him the Fa - ther gave us. _____ I - de - o - o - o, i - de -

o - o - o, I - de - o glo - ri - a in ex - cel - sis De - o.

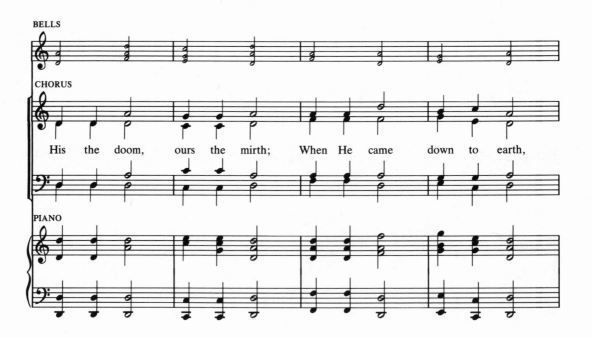

BELLS

CHORUS

His the doom, ours the mirth; When He came down to earth,

PIANO

76

Beth - le - hem saw His birth; Ox and ass be - side Him,

From the cold would hide Him. _____ I - de - o - o - o, I - de -

o - o - o, I - de - o glo - ri - a in ex - cel - sis De - o.

NOVA! NOVA!

The refrain contains an interesting play on words. "Nova" means "news." "Ave," the Latin word for "hail," is "Eva" spelled backwards. "Ave fit ex Eva" means "Ave is made from Eva." This expresses the mediæval belief that Eva's (Eve's) 'sin,' shared by all women, was forgiven when the Angel Gabriel greeted Mary with the news that she would bear the Son of God. "Nova! Nova!" is an example of a macaronic carol, illustrating the inclusion of the vernacular with church Latin.

15th century mss.
Glasgow, Scotland

at a steady tempo ♩.=116

*Bells needed: F G B♭

3. When the maiden heard tell of this,
She was full sore abashed y-wis,
And weened that she had done amiss;
   Nova, nova! . . . &c.

4. Then said the angel: Dread not thou,
For ye be conceived with great virtue
Whose name shall be called Jesu;
   Nova, nova! . . . &c.

5. Then said the maiden: Verily,
I am your servant right truly;
Ecce, ancilla Domini;
   Nova, nova! . . . &c.

79

SING WE NOËL

This early French tune makes a joyous processional, with its descant for high voices or instruments and handbells. The English text was written by Susan Cooper for The Christmas Revels.

anon. 16th century French
arr. Marshall Barron

moving along joyously ♩=52

DESCANT SUNG TO LAST VERSE

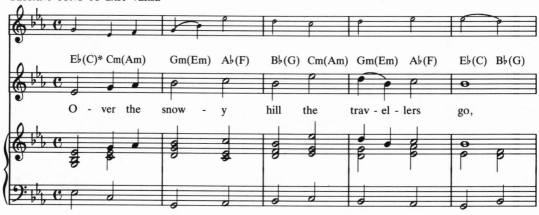

Eb(C)* Cm(Am) Gm(Em) Ab(F) Bb(G) Cm(Am) Gm(Em) Ab(F) Eb(C) Bb(G)

O - ver the snow - y hill the trav - el - lers go,

Eb(C) Ab(F) Cm(Am) Fm(Dm) Eb(C) Bb(G) Eb(C) Cm(Am)

Sing we No - ël, No - ël, ___ No - ël! Call - ing to

*(Capo III)

wake   the   sleep - ing   town __ be - low,   Sing   we   No -

él,   No - él, ___ No - él! _____ "We   bring   you

joy   up - on __ this   star, __ That   breaks   the   dark-ness from a -

Bb(G) Eb(C) Ab(F) Cm(Am)Fm(Dm) Eb(C) Bb(G) Eb(C)

far; Sing we No - ël, No - ël,___ No - ël."

2. Nearer they come, their voices clear and high,
Sing we Noël, Noël, Noël!
Calling their promise through the frosty sky,
Sing we Noël, Noël, Noël!
"We bring you love, the faithful light
Of dawn that comes to end the night;
Sing we Noël, Noël, Noël!"

3. Sing then and join them as they go their way,
Sing we Noël, Noël, Noël!
Crossing the world with greetings for this day,
Sing we Noël, Noël, Noël!
"We bring you peace, to cherish long,
And let tomorrow hear our song:
Sing we Noël, Noël, Noël!"

WEXFORD CAROL

This carol comes from county Wexford, where a mummers' play is performed annually at the Christmas season. This spirited carol makes a fine processional.

trad. Irish
arr. John Edmunds

lively, but unhurried ♩=84

Good peo-ple all, this Christ-mas-time, Con-sid-er well ___ and bear in mind What our good ___ God for us has done In send-ing His ___ be-lov-ed Son. O

let us all __ both sing and pray To __ God __ with love __ this

1. 2. 3 *al Segno*

Christ-mas Day; In Beth-le-hem that Christ-mas morn There

was a bles-sed Mes - si - ah born. __

2. Near
3. With

At - tend - ing ___ on the Lord of Life Who

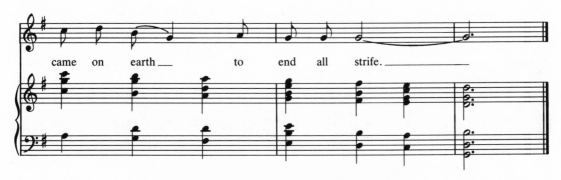

came on earth ___ to end all strife. ___

2. Near Bethlehem did shepherds keep
Their flocks of lambs and feeding sheep;
To whom God's angels did appear,
Which put the shepherds in great fear.
"Prepare and go," the angels said,
"To Bethlehem, be not afraid;
For there you'll find, this happy morn,
A princely babe, sweet Jesus born."

3. With thankful heart and joyful mind
The shepherds went the Babe to find
And as God's angel had foretold
They did our Saviour Christ behold.
Within a manger He was laid,
And by His side the Virgin Maid
Attending on the Lord of Life
Who came on earth to end all strife.

THE BABE OF BETHLEHEM

This strong Dorian tune is widespread in oral tradition, with variants found in ballads, folksongs and hymns. The words are as characteristic of the folk as the melody, and might well have been sung in one of the mediæval miracle plays.

The doubling of the octave in the tenor (melody) and the soprano parts was encouraged by the colonial composers of New England. Such singing sounds best unaccompanied.

with a strong rhythmic sweep ♩.=80

Southern Harmony, shape-note hymnal
New Haven, Connecticut 1835

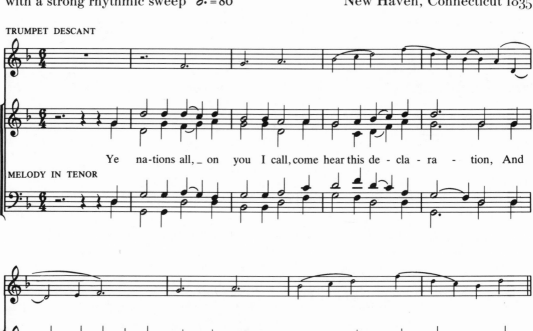

TRUMPET DESCANT

MELODY IN TENOR

Ye na-tions all,_ on you I call, come hear this de - cla - ra - tion, And

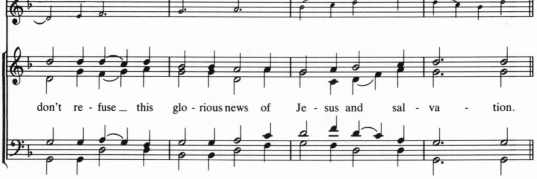

don't re - fuse _ this glo - rious news of Je - sus and sal - va - tion.

To roy-al Jews came first the news of Christ the great Mes - si - ah, As
was fore-told by proph-ets old, I - sa - iah, Jer - e - mi - ah.

2. His parents poor in earthly store, to entertain the stranger,
They found no bed to lay His head but in the ox's manger.
No royal things, as used by kings, were seen by those that found Him;
But in the hay the stranger lay, with swaddling bands around Him.

3. On that same night a glorious light to shepherds there appeared,
Bright angels came in shining flame, they saw and greatly feared.
The angels said, "Be not afraid, although we much alarm you,
We do appear good news to bear, as now we will inform you."

4. When this was said, straightway was made a glorious sound from heaven,
Each flaming tongue an anthem sung, "To men a Saviour's given."
In Jesus' name, the glorious theme, we elevate our voices;
At Jesus' birth be peace on earth, meanwhile all heaven rejoices.

RITUAL SONGS

APPLE TREE WASSAIL

This wassail ritual, performed at night by firelight, ensured new growth in the fruit trees. Bits of lambs' wool, dipped in old cider, were affixed to the branches of the trees. The singing and dancing was punctuated with loud banging noises and shouts to drive away evil spirits. This variant from Somerset reflects the early origin of the *carol,* which involved taking hands and singing while dancing in a ring or around a bush or May tree.

trad. English
arr. Marshall Barron

with a swing ♩.=96

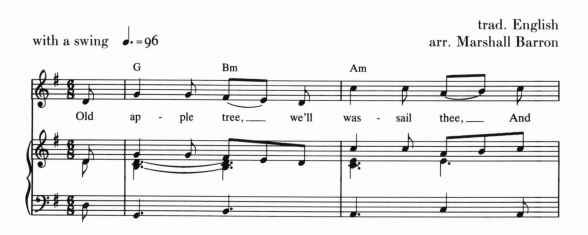

Old ap - ple tree, __ we'll was - sail thee, __ And

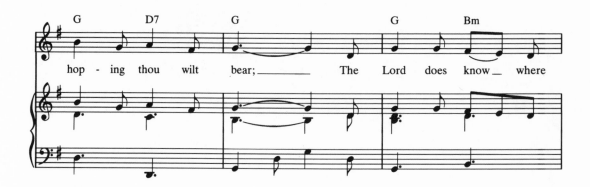

hop - ing thou wilt bear; _____ The Lord does know _ where

Am   G   D7   G

we shall be To be mer - ry an - o - ther year._____ To____

G   Am   D7   G

blow well and to bear well, And so mer - ry let us

D   G   Bm   Am

be;_____ Let ev - 'ry man__ drink up his cup:__ Here's

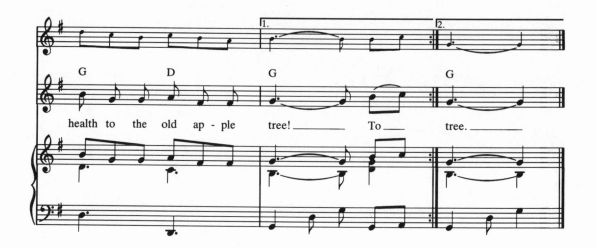

health to the old ap - ple tree! _____ To ____ tree. _____

Shouts at the conclusion: *Capfulls! Hatfulls! Baskets full!*
Bushels full! Barrels full! Barn floors full!
—and a little heap under the stairs!

ABBOTS BROMLEY
HORN DANCE TUNE

In the Christmas Revels, this haunting tune is played for the ancient ceremony of "deer running," once a mid-winter ritual dance of the hunt, which is still danced annually at the village of Abbots Bromley, Staffordshire. Eight men, holding reindeer antlers above their heads, and accompanied by the traditional folk Fool, the Man-Woman, Hobby Horse and Boy Hunter, process through the village and outlying farms, "bringing in the luck."

with a steady pulse ♩.=84

trad. English

CORNISH WASSAIL

The village "waits" went about from house to house, from farm to farm, bringing good luck in with their singing.

with a great swing $\text{\textonehalf} = 60$

trad. English
arr. Jerome Epstein

2. Here at your door, we already do stand,
The jolly warzail boys with a bowl in our hand.

> *With our warzail, warzail, warzail,*
> *and joy come to our jolly warzail!*

3. This ancient old house we will kindly salute.
It is an old custom you need not dispute.

> *With our warzail . . . &c.*

4. We hope that your apple trees prosper and bear,
And bring forth good tidings when we come next year.

> *With our warzail . . . &c.*

5. We hope that your barley will prosper and grow,
That you may have plenty and more to bestow.

> *With our warzail . . . &c.*

GLOUCESTERSHIRE WASSAIL

The word "wassail" comes from the Anglo-Saxon "wes hal," meaning "be whole"—a greeting for "good health!" The wassailers travelled from house to house singing, with a wassail cup which their hosts were expected to fill.

trad. English
arr. Marshall Barron

with a strong swing ♩.=63

Was - sail, was - sail,__ all o - ver the town,__ Our bread it is

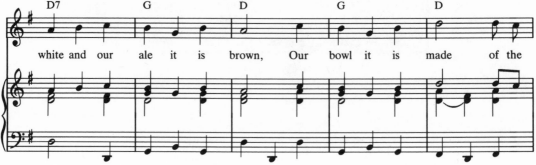

white and our ale it is brown, Our bowl it is made of the

96

white ma - ple tree, With the was - sail-ing bowl we'll drink _ to thee.

2. Here's a health to the ox and to his right eye;
Pray God send our master a good Christmas pie,
A good Christmas pie that may we all see,
With the wassailing bowl we'll drink to thee.

3. Here's a health to the cow and to her long tail;
Pray God send our master a good cask of ale;
A good cask of ale that may we all see,
With the wassailing bowl we'll drink to thee.

4. Come butler, come fill us a bowl of the best,
Then I pray that your soul in heaven may rest;
But if you do bring us a bowl of the small,
May the devil take butler, bowl and all!

5. Then here's to the maid in the lily-white smock,
Who tripped to the door and slipped back the lock;
Who tripped to the door, and pulled back the pin,
For to let these jolly wassailers walk in.

> *Wassail, wassail, all over the town,*
> *Our bread it is white and our ale it is brown;*
> *Our bowl it is made of the white maple tree;*
> *With the wassailing bowl we'll drink to thee.*

GOWER WASSAIL

A spirited carol from the Gower peninsula, which we learned from the great traditional singer Philip Tanner.

trad. Welsh
arr. Jerome Epstein

in strict rhythm ♩=138

A - was-sail, a - was-sail, through-out all this town. Our __

cup it is white __ and our ale it is brown. Our __ was-sail is __

made of the good - ale and true, Some _ nut - meg and

gin - ger, it's the best we can brew. _ Fol the dol, fol the dol - de -

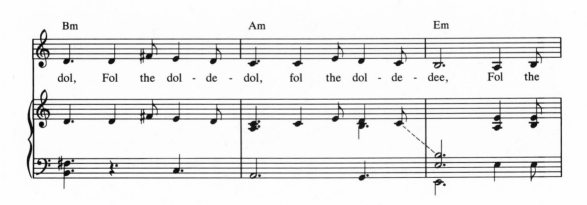

dol, Fol the dol - de - dol, fol the dol - de - dee, Fol the

99

der - o, fol the dad - dy, Sing tu - re - lye - do!

BELLS* *(last verse)*

We __ know by the __ moon that we are not too soon, We __

know by the sky ___ that we are not too high, We __

*Bells needed: C D E F G A B c d e

100

know by the ___ stars that we are ___ not too far, We ___

know by the ground ___ that we are with - in sound. ___ Fol the

dol, fol the dol - de - dol, Fol the dol - de - dol, fol the dol - de -

dee, Fol the der - o, fol the dad - dy, Sing tu - re - lye $_2$ - do!

2. Our wassail is made of an elderberry bough
And so, my good neighbour, we'll drink unto thou;
Besides all of that, you'll have apples in store,
Pray let us come in for it's cold by the door.

> Fol the dol, fol the dol-de-dol,
> Fol the dol-de-dol, fol the dol-de-dee,
> Fol the der-o, fol the daddy,
> Sing tu-re-lye-do!

3. We hope that your apple trees prosper and bear
So we may have cider when we call next year,
And where you've one barrel I hope you'll have ten,
So we can have cider when we call again.

> Fol the dol . . . &c.

4. We know by the moon that we are not too soon,
We know by the sky that we are not too high,
We know by the stars that we are not too far,
We know by the ground that we are within sound.

> Fol the dol . . . &c.

PLEASE TO SEE THE KING

A traditional carol from Pembrokeshire, South Wales, commemorating the ritual King-killing of the wren on St. Stephen's Day, December 26.

trad. Welsh
arr. Jerome Epstein

quietly and decisively ♩=84

SOPRANO

ALTO AND
TENOR

Joy,___ health, love and peace be___ all here in this___

BASS

By your leave

place. By___ your leave we___ will sing con - cern - ing___ our___ King.

By your leave

2. Our King is well dressed, in silks of the best,
In ribbons so rare, no king can compare.

3. We have travelled many miles, over hedges and stiles,
In search of our King, unto you we bring.

4. Old Christmas is past, Twelfth Night is the last,
And we bid you adieu, great joy to the new.

KENTUCKY WASSAIL

Among the folksongs transplanted from Britain to the Southern Appalachian Mountains is this wassail carol, collected by John Jacob Niles, which took on the American quality and dance characteristics of that region. Some stanzas are similar to the Somerset wassail song.

trad. American
arr. Marshall Barron

vigorously ♩=88

Was - sail, was - sail, all ___ o - ver the town, Our

cup is white and our ale is brown. The ___ cup ___ is made ___ from the

old oak tree, And the ale __ is made __ in __ Ken - tuck - y, So it's

joy   be   to   you   and   a   jol - ly   was - sail!

2. Oh, good man and good wife, are you within?
Pray lift the latch and let us come in.
We see you a-sitting at the boot o' the fire,
Not a-thinkin' of us in the mud and the mire,
So it's joy be to you and a jolly wassail!

3. There was an old maid and she lived in a house,
And she had for a pet a tiny wee mouse,
Oh, the house had a stove and the house was warm,
And a little bit of liquor won't do no harm,
So it's joy be to you and a jolly wassail!

4. Oh, a man in York drank his sack from a pail,
But all we ask is a wee wassail.
Oh, husband and wife, alack, we part,
God bless this house from the bottom of our heart,
So it's joy be to you and a jolly wassail!

SOMERSET WASSAIL

Cecil Sharp collected this carol early this century from the Drayton wassailers in Somerset. Sharp thought that the "great dog of Langport" was a reference to the Danes whose invasion of Langport in the ninth century is not yet forgotten.

trad. English
arr. Jerome Epstein

with vigor ♩=84

Was-sail ___ and was-sail, all ___ o-ver the town! The cup ___ it is white and the ale ___ it is

*(Capo I)

106

107

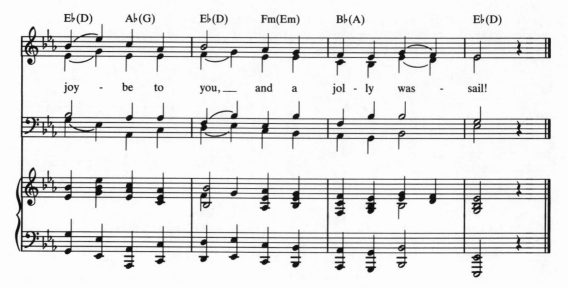

joy - be to you, — and a jol - ly was - sail!

2. O master and missus, are you all within?
Pray open the door and let us come in.
O master and missus a-sitting by the fire,
Pray think on us poor travellers, a-travelling in the mire:

> For it's your wassail, and it's our wassail!
> And it's joy be to you, and a jolly wassail!

3. O where is the maid, with the silver-headed pin,
To open the door, and let us come in?
O master and missus, it is our desire:
A good loaf and cheese, and a toast by the fire:

> For it's your wassail, etc.

4. There was an old man, and he had an old cow,
And how for to keep her he didn't know how;
He built up a barn for to keep his cow warm.
And a drop or two of cider will do us no harm:

> No harm, boys, harm; no harm, boys, harm;
> And a drop or two of cider will do us no harm.

5. The girt dog of Langport he burnt his long tail,
And this is the night we go singing wassail.
O master and missus, now we must be gone;
God bless all in this house till we do come again;

> For it's your wassail, etc.

THE HOLLY AND THE IVY

An unusual variant collected in Herefordshire by Pat Shaw and Maud Karpeles in 1952. The subject is probably of pagan origin, and symbolized the male (holly) and female (ivy) principles in nature. A suggestion of sun worship and animal worship is found in the refrain.

trad. English
arr. Marshall Barron

with an easy swing ♩.=69

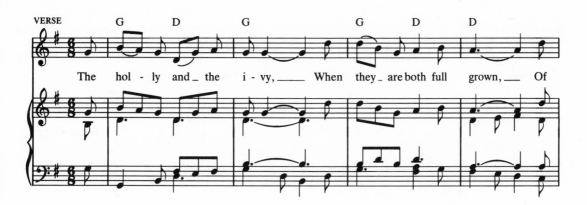

The hol - ly and the i - vy, ___ When they are both full grown, ___ Of

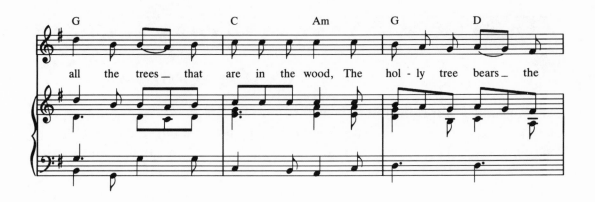

all the trees__ that are in the wood, The hol - ly tree bears__ the

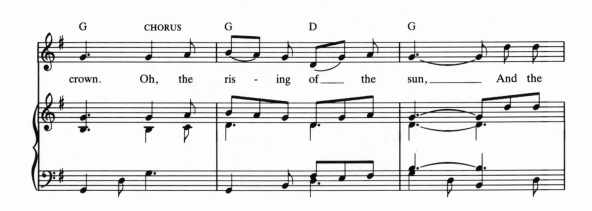

crown. Oh, the ris - ing of__ the sun,_____ And the

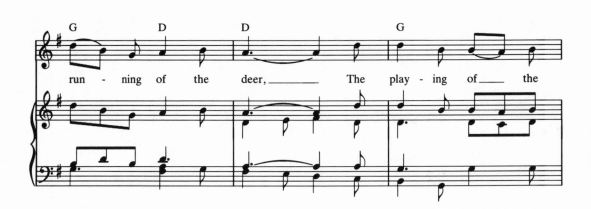

run - ning of the deer,_____ The play - ing of__ the

merry or-gan, Sweet sing-ing all in the choir.

2. The holly bears a blossom
As white as the lily flower,
And Mary bore sweet Jesus Christ
To be our sweet Saviour.

Oh, the rising of the sun
And the running of the deer,
The playing of the merry organ,
Sweet singing all in the choir.

3. The holly bears a berry
As red as any blood,
And Mary bore sweet Jesus Christ
To do poor sinners good.

Oh, the rising of the sun . . . &c.

4. The holly bears a prickle
As sharp as any thorn,
And Mary bore sweet Jesus Christ
On Christmas Day in the morn.

Oh, the rising of the sun . . . &c.

5. The holly and the ivy,
When they are both full grown,
Of all the trees that are in the wood
The holly tree bears the crown.

Oh, the rising of the sun . . . &c.

SUSSEX MUMMERS' CAROL

Collected by Lucy Broadwood in the late nineteenth century, this traditional carol was sung by the mummers, or "tipteers," as part of the folk play in Horsham, Sussex.

trad. English
arr. Marshall Barron

joyously ♩=76

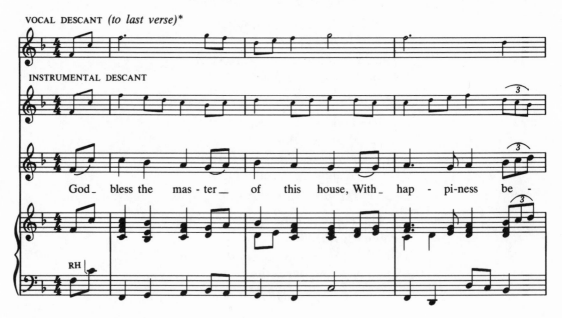

God__ bless the mas-ter__ of this house, With__ hap - pi-ness be -

*Vocal descant should be sung on vowel *ah* throughout, or with text for last verse.

side, Where - e'er his bo - dy rides or _ walks, _ His God must be his guide, _____ his God _____ must _ be _____ his guide.

2. God bless the mistress of this house,
With gold chain round her breast;
Where-e'er her body sleeps or wakes,
Lord send her soul to rest,
Lord send her soul to rest.

3. God bless your house, your children too,
Your cattle and your store;
The Lord increase you day by day,
And send you more and more,
And send you more and more.

THE BOAR'S HEAD CAROL

This carol has been sung at Queen's College, Oxford, since the seventeenth century, as the celebrated dish is borne into the dining hall. An early version of a boar's head carol was first printed in 1521 by Wynkyn de Worde.

anon. English
arr. Elizabeth Posten

CHORUS   (Inst.)

Ca - put a - pri   de - fe - ro,   Red - dens lau - des Do - mi - no.

ALTERNATIVE CHORUS FOR LAST VERSE

Ca - put   a - pri __ de - fe - ro,   Red - dens lau - des   Do - mi - no.

MELODY

2. The boar's head, as I understand,
Is the rarest dish in all the land
When thus bedecked with a gay garland,
Let us *servire cantico:*

> *Caput apri defero,*
> *Reddens laudes Domino.*

3. Our steward hath provided this
In honour of the King of bliss,
Which on this day to be served is,
In Reginensi atrio:

> *Caput apri defero . . . &c.*

Quot . . . "so many as are in the feast"
Caput . . . "The boar's head I bring, giving praises to God"
Servire . . . "Let us serve with a song"
In Reginensi . . . "In the Queen's Hall"

CHILDREN'S SONGS

AS I SAT ON A SUNNY BANK

A well-known children's skipping tune in new garb as a variant of the carol "I Saw Three Ships Come Sailing In."

trad. English
arr. Marshall Barron

spritely ♩. = 104

On Christ - mas Day in the morn - ing.

G   D   G   D   G

sun - ny bank On Christ - mas Day in the morn - ing.

2. I saw three ships come sailing by,
Come sailing by, come sailing by,
I saw three ships come sailing by
On Christmas Day in the morning.

3. And who was in those ships all three,
Those ships all three, . . . &c.

4. 'Twas Joseph and his fair lady,
His fair lady, . . . &c.

5. Then he did whistle and she did sing,
And she did sing, . . . &c.

6. And all the bells on earth shall ring,
On earth shall ring, . . . &c.

CHILDREN, GO
WHERE I SEND THEE

The cumulative structure of this carol reminds one of the ancient Hebrew song *"Chad Gadyo,"* sung at Passover.

trad. Black American
arr. Marshall Barron

spirited ♩= 100

Chil - dren, go where I send thee. How will you send me? I will send you one by one 'cause

*(Capo III)

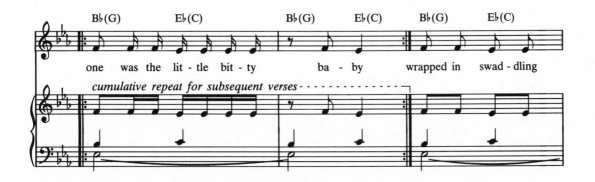

one was the lit - tle bit - ty ba - by wrapped in swad - dling

cumulative repeat for subsequent verses - - - - - - - - - - - - - -

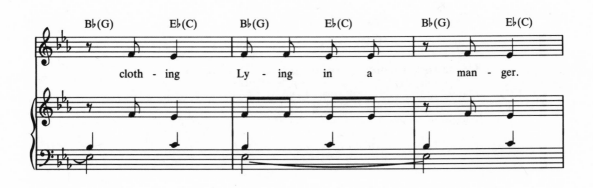

cloth - ing Ly - ing in a man - ger.

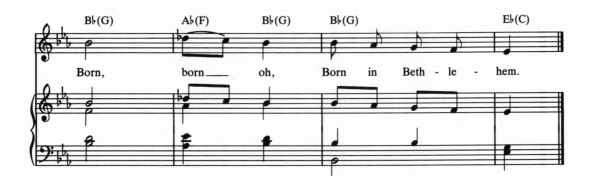

Born, born____ oh, Born in Beth - le - hem.

Children, go where I send thee.
How will you send me?
I will send you two by two
'Cause two were Paul and Silas,
One was the little bitty baby,
Wrapped in swaddling clothing,
Lying in a manger.
Born, born — oh,
Born in Bethlehem.

. . .'Cause three were the Hebrew children,
Two were Paul and Silas,
One was the little bitty baby . . . &c.

. . .'Cause four were the four come a-knocking at the door . . . &c.

. . .'Cause five were the gospel preachers . . . &c.

. . .'Cause six were the six that couldn't get fixed . . . &c.

. . .'Cause seven were the seven that went to heaven . . . &c.

. . .'Cause eight were the eight that stood at the gate . . . &c.

. . .'Cause nine were the nine got left behind . . . &c.

. . .'Cause ten were the ten commandments . . . &c.

DAME, GET UP
AND BAKE YOUR PIES

A circle dance in which little children can pantomime the words and skip to the refrain. The tune is related to "Greensleeves" and the carol "What Child Is This."

trad. English
arr. Marshall Barron

briskly ♩.= 120

Dame, get up and bake your pies, bake your pies, bake your pies.

Dame, get up and bake your pies ___ on Christ - mas Day in the morn - ing.

*(Capo V)

2. Dame, what makes your ducks to cry,
Ducks to cry, ducks to cry?
Dame, what makes your ducks to cry
On Christmas Day in the morning?

3. Their wings are cut, they cannot fly,
Cannot fly, cannot fly . . . &c.

4. Dame, what makes your maidens lie,
Maidens lie, maidens lie . . . &c.

5. Dame, get up and bake your pies,
Bake your pies, bake your pies . . . &c.

THE CAROL OF THE BIRDS

Young children can freely dance and mime the birds as they sing this song.

John Jacob Niles
arr. Marshall Barron

lightly ♩.= 88

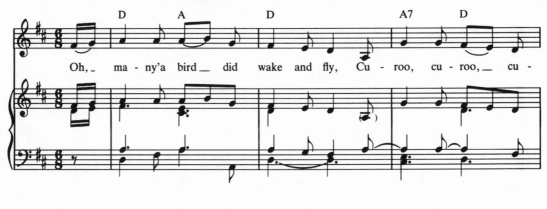

Oh, _ ma-ny'a bird_ did wake and fly, Cu - roo, cu - roo, _ cu -

roo, _____ Oh, _ ma-ny'a bird_ did wake and fly To the man-ger bed with

2. The lark, the dove, the red bird came
Curoo, curoo, curoo,
The lark, the dove, the red bird came
And worshipped there in Jesus' name,
On Christmas Day in the morning,
Curoo, curoo, curoo,
Curoo, curoo, curoo.

3. The owl was there, his eyes so wide,
Curoo . . . &c.
The owl was there, his eyes so wide
As he did sit at Mary's side,
On Christmas Day in the morning,
Curoo . . . &c.

THE FRIENDLY BEASTS

A quiet carol in which young children can act out the Christmas animals. (See "Orientis Partibus" — "Song of the Ass" — for the original mediæval version of this carol in a different mode and meter.)

anon. French
arr. Marshall Barron

smoothly ♩. = 48

Je - sus, our broth - er, kind and good, Was hum - bly born in a sta - ble rude; And the friend - ly beasts a -

*(Capo III)

126

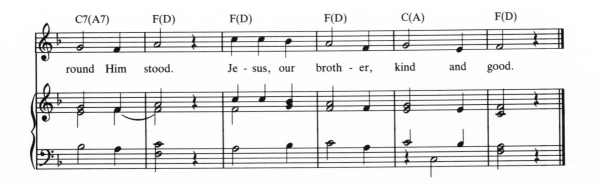

round Him stood. Je - sus, our broth - er, kind and good.

2. "I," said the Donkey, shaggy and brown,
"I carried His mother up hill and down;
I carried His mother to Bethlehem town."
"I," said the Donkey, shaggy and brown.

3. "I," said the Cow, all white and red,
"I gave Him my manger for His bed;
I gave Him my hay to pillow His head."
"I," said the Cow, all white and red.

4. "I," said the Sheep, with the curly horn,
"I gave Him my wool for His blanket warm;
He wore my coat on Christmas morn."
"I," said the Sheep, with the curly horn.

5. "I," said the Dove, from the rafters high,
"Cooed Him to sleep that He should not cry;
We cooed Him to sleep, my mate and I."
"I," said the Dove, from the rafters high.

6. Thus every beast by some glad spell,
In the stable dark was glad to tell
Of the gift he gave Emmanuel,
The gift he gave Emmanuel.

THE WREN SONG

December 26, St. Stephen's Day, is still recognized traditionally in Ireland with this ancient song about the wren, the magical bringer of luck to the New Year. A group of children disguised and carrying a little caged effigy, vigorously sing this song from door to door.

trad. Irish
arr. Marshall Barron

with plenty of gusto ♩. = 112

The wren, the wren, the king of all birds, Saint

Ste-phen's Day was caught in the firs; Al-though he was lit-tle, his

hon - or was great, Jump up, me lads, and give us a treat!

PERCUSSION

2. We followed the wren three miles or more,
Three miles or more, three miles or more,
Through hedges and ditches and heaps of snow,
At six o'clock in the morning.

3. Rolley, Rolley, where's your nest?
It's in the bush that I love best,
It's in the bush, the holly tree,
Where all the boys do follow me.

4. As I went out to hunt and all,
I met a wren upon the wall,
Up with me wattle and gave him a fall,
And brought him here to show you all.

5. I have a little box under me arm,
A tuppence or penny'll do it no harm,
For we are the boys that came your way
To bring in the wren on St. Stephen's Day!

THERE WAS A PIG WENT
OUT TO DIG

An old agrarian mummers' carol from Bedfordshire, linking the Christmas season with the cycle of planting and harvesting. At one time this carol was mimed by men of the village. It is one of many carols and legends concerning the importance of animals at Christmas time.

trad. English
arr. Marshall Barron

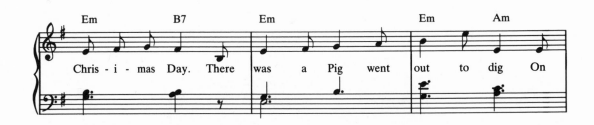

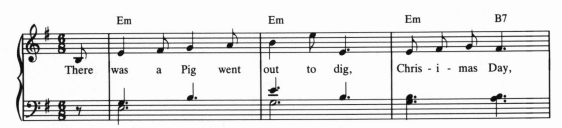

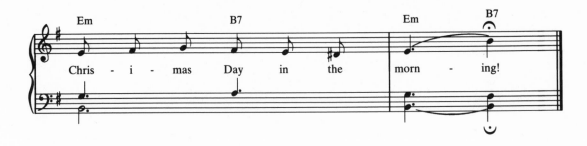

2. There was a Cow went out to plough,
Chris-i-mas Day, Chris-i-mas Day,
There was a Cow went out to plough
On Chris-i-mas Day in the morning!

3. There was a sparrow went out to harrow,
. . . &c.

4. There was a crow went out to sow,
. . . &c.

5. There was a sheep went out to reap,
. . . &c.

6. There was a drake went out to rake,
. . . &c.

7. There was a minnow went out to winnow,
. . . &c.

Goody Gruntum's Farm

WE'VE BEEN AWHILE A-WANDERING

A wassail song from Yorkshire, sung by the street *waits* from house to house on Christmas Eve.

trad. English
arr. Marshall Barron

at a lilting pace ♩.=96

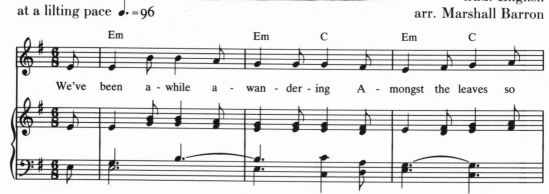

We've been a-while a-wan-der-ing A-mongst the leaves so

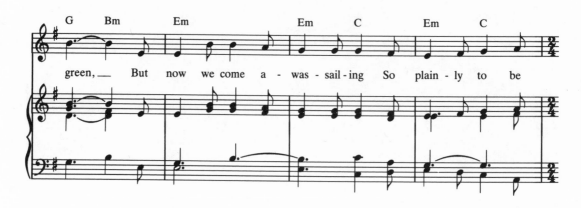

green,— But now we come a-was-sail-ing So plain-ly to be

seen; For it's Christ-mas time, when we tra-vel far and near; May God bless you and send you a hap-py New Year.

2. We are not daily beggars
That beg from door to door;
We are your neighbor's children,
For we've been here before;

*For it's Christmas time,
   when we travel far and near;
May God bless you and send you
   a happy New Year.*

3. Good master and good mistress,
While you're sitting by the fire,
Pray think of us poor children
That's wandered in the mire;

For it's Christmas time . . . &c.

4. Bring us out a table
And spread it with a cloth,
Bring us out a mouldy cheese
And some of your Christmas loaf;

For it's Christmas time . . . &c.

5. Call up the butler of this house,
Likewise the mistress too,
And all the little children
That round the table go;

For it's Christmas time . . . &c.

WHAT SHALL I GIVE TO THE CHILD?

This dance noël from Catalonia, with its local text, perhaps brings us closer to Bethlehem than the winter snows of a New England Christmas! Light percussion can be added by children with tambourine, maracas or small drums as they sing "Tamp-a-tamp-tamp" in contrast to the smoothness of the verses.

trad. Spanish
arr. Marshall Barron

gently and smoothly ♩. = 46

What shall I give to the Child in the man - ger?

What shall I give to the beau - ti - ful Boy?

Grapes I will give to Him, hang - ing in clus - ters,

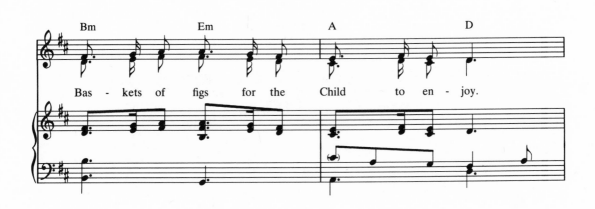

Bas - kets of figs for the Child to en - joy.

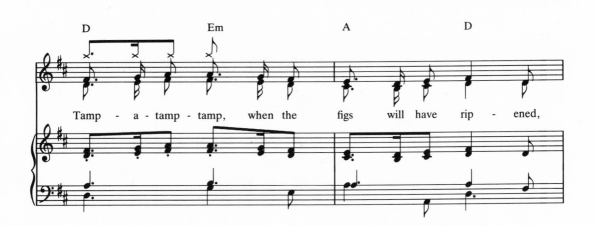

Tamp - a - tamp - tamp, when the figs will have rip - ened,

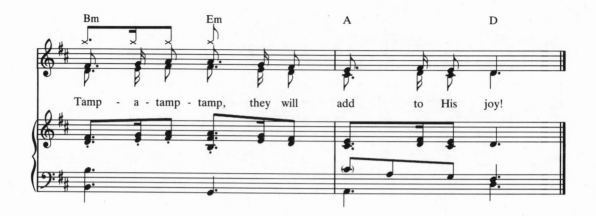

Tamp - a - tamp - tamp, they will add to His joy!

2. What shall I give to the Child in the manger?
What shall I give to the beautiful Boy?
Garlands of flowers to twine in His fingers,
Cherries so big for the Child to enjoy.
Tamp-a-tamp-tamp, when the cherries have ripened,
Tamp-a-tamp-tamp, they will add to His joy!

GLORY TO THE MOUNTAIN

A children's game-song collected by Margaret Hodgkin in Harlem, New York City, 1970.

walking tempo

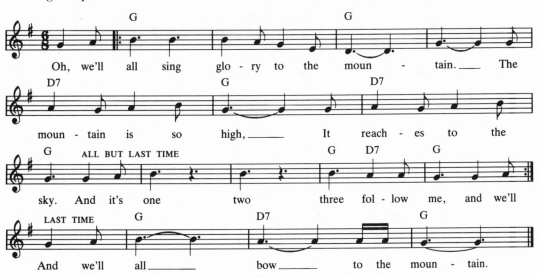

Oh, we'll all sing glo-ry to the moun - tain.___ The moun - tain is so high,___ It reach - es to the sky. And it's one two three fol - low me, and we'll And we'll all___ bow___ to the moun - tain.

Directions: A circle is made holding hands and singing, while moving in a clockwise direction. A leader is outside the circle going around in the opposite direction. When the song says, "one, two, three . . ." the leader taps three of the children, who leave the center circle and follow the leader in the outside circle.

When one child is left in the center, the others all stop moving and face into the middle, bowing to the *Mountain,* as they sing the end part of the song. The "mountain" becomes the new leader.

137

HERE WE COME A-WASSAILING

There are many variants of this folksong which is sung by the "waits" as they go carolling from door to door to bring luck for the New Year to their neighbors.

trad. English
arr. Marshall Barron

cheerfully ♩.=80

Here we come a - was - sail - ing A - mong the leaves so green, ___

Here we come a - wand - 'ring So fair ___ to be seen;

CHORUS

Love and joy come to you, And to you your was - sail

too, And God bless you and send_ you a hap - py New

Year, And God send you a hap - py New_ Year.

2. We are not daily beggars
That beg from door to door,
We are your neighbor's children
Whom you have seen before.

> *Love and joy come to you,*
> *And to you your wassail too,*
> *And God bless you and send you a happy New Year,*
> *And God send you a happy New Year.*

3. God bless the master of this house,
Likewise the mistress too,
And all the little children
That round the table go.

> *Love and joy come to you . . . &c.*

ROUNDS

A CHRISTMAS ROUND

This is a most effective round, very simple in structure, but composed in such a way as to make it sound complex and sonorous when all the parts are heard together.

Pat Shaw, 1978

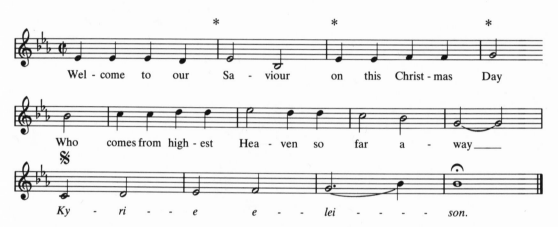

Wel - come to our Sa - viour on this Christ - mas Day

Who comes from high - est Hea - ven so far a - way___

Ky - ri - e e - lei - son.

Parts enter in this order: soprano, tenor, alto, bass.
Final time: soprano and tenor sing to last note, and hold until alto finishes.

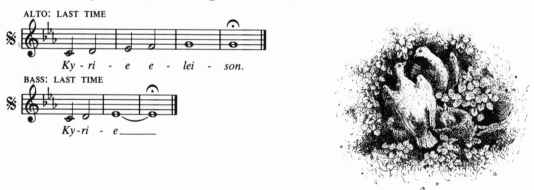

ALTO: LAST TIME

Ky - ri - e e - lei - son.

BASS: LAST TIME

Ky - ri - e___

Note on singing the rounds: asterisks indicate where voices enter. Fermatas indicate where voices end together.

OKEN LEAVES

Found in Thomas Ravenscroft's collection *Pammelia,* published in 1609.

Ok - en leaves in the mer - ry wood so wild. When will

you grow green - a? Ma - ry Maid, and thou be with child,

Lul - la - by may'st thou sing - a: Lul - la, lul - la - by,

lul - la, lul - la, lul - la - by, Lul - la - by may'st thou sing - a.

DONA NOBIS PACEM

Do-na no-bis pa - cem, pa-cem, do - na no - bis pa - cem.

Do - na no - bis pa-cem, do-na no-bis pa - cem.

Do - na no - bis pa-cem, do-na no-bis pa - cem.

PEACE ROUND

The tune is an old English canon.

words by Jean Ritchie

What a good - ly thing If the chil - dren of the world

Could dwell to - geth - er In_____ peace.

SHALOM CHAVERIM

Sha - lom, cha - ve - rim, sha - lom, cha - ve - rim, Sha - lom, sha -

lom L' - hit - ra - ot l' - hit - ra - ot Sha - lom, sha - lom.

ALLELUIA ROUND

William Boyce

Al - - - - le - - - - lu - - - -

* Al - le - lu - ia, Al - le - lu - ia, ___ Al - le - lu -

* Al - - le - lu - ia, Al - le - lu -

ia, Al - le - lu - - - - - ia.

ia, Al - - le - lu - ia, Al - - le - lu - ia.

ia. Al - le - lu - ia, Al - le - lu - ia.

INDEX OF TITLES

A Christmas Round 142
Abbots Bromley Horn Dance Tune 93
Alle Psallite cum Luya 2
Alleluia Round, The 145
Apple Tree Wassail 90
As I Sat on a Sunny Bank 118
Babe of Bethlehem, The 86
Bells in the High Tower 8
Boar's Head Carol, The 114
Brightest and Best 4
Carol of the Birds, The 124
Cherry Tree Carol, The 38
Children, Go Where I Send Thee 120
Christ Child's Lullaby, The 40
Christmas Eve Is Here 10
Cornish Wassail 94
Dame, Get Up and Bake Your Pies . . . 123
Deck the Hall 12
Dona Nobis Pacem 143
Exultation 62
First Nowell, The 42
Friendly Beasts, The 126
Glory to the Mountain 137
Gloucestershire Wassail 96
Go, Tell It on the Mountain 14
Gower Wassail 98
Green Grow'th the Holly 19
Here We Come A-wassailing 138
Holly and the Ivy, The 109
Huron Indian Carol 16
I Saw Three Ships 64
Jolly Old Hawk 20

Kentucky Wassail 104
King Herod and the Cock 29
Lord of the Dance, The 46
Mary Had a Baby 24
Masters in This Hall 66
Milford 26
Moon Shines Bright, The 49
Nova! Nova! 79
O Little Town of Bethlehem
    (Forest Green) 30
Oken Leaves 143
On Christmas Night 32
Orientis Partibus 73
Peace Round 144
Personent Hodie (On This Day) 74
Please to See the King 103
Shalom Chaverim 144
Silent Night 34
Sing We Noël 80
Somerset Wassail 106
Star in the East 36
Sussex Mummers' Carol 112
There Was a Pig Went Out to Dig 130
Truth from Above, The 7
Truth Sent from Above, The 45
Twelve Days of Christmas, The 50
We've Been Awhile A-wandering 132
Wexford Carol 83
What Shall I Give to the Child? 134
While Shepherds Watched 55
Wondrous Love 58
Wren Song, The 128

INDEX OF FIRST LINES

Alle psallite cum luya. 2
Alleluia. 145
As I sat on a sunny bank. 118
Bells in the high tower. 8
Children, go where I send thee 120
Christmas Eve is here 10
Come away to the skies. 62
Dame, get up and bake your pies 123
Deck the hall. 12
Dona nobis pacem 143
From the East the donkey came 73
Go, tell it on the mountain 14
God bless the master of this house. 112
Good people all, this Christmastime 83
Green grow'th the holly. 19
Hail the blest morn (Brightest and Best) . 4
Hail the blest morn (Star in the East) . . . 36
Here we come a-wassailing. 138
I danced in the morning when the world
    was begun 46
I saw three ships come sailing in 64
If angels sung a Saviour's birth 26
Jesus, our brother, kind and good 126
Jolly old hawk and his wings were grey . 20
Joy, health, love and peace 103
Mary had a baby 24
Masters in this hall. 66
My love, my pride, my treasure-oh. 40
Now Christmas is com-en and New
    Year begin 94
Nova! nova! Ave fit ex Eva. 79
O, little town of Bethlehem. 30
Oh, many a bird did wake and fly 124
Oh, we'll all sing glory to the mountain 137
Oken leaves in the merry wood so wilde 143
Old apple tree, we'll wassail thee. 90
On Christmas night all people sing 32

On the first day of Christmas 50
On this day earth shall ring. 74
Orientis partibus. 73
Over the snowy hill the travellers go. . . 80
Personent hodie 74
Shalom chaverim 144
Silent night, holy night 34
The boar's head in hand bear I 114
The first Nowell the angel did say. 42
The holly and the ivy 109
The moon shines bright. 49
The wassail, the wassail, throughout all
    the town (Gower) 98
The wren, the wren, the king of all
    birds 128
There was a pig went out to dig. 130
There was a star in David's land 29
This is the truth sent from above
    (Shropshire). 45
This is the truth sent from above
    (Herefordshire) 7
'Twas in the moon of wintertime 16
Wassail, and wassail, all over the town
    (Somerset) 106
Wassail, wassail, all over the town
    (Kentucky). 104
Wassail, wassail, all over the town
    (Gloucestershire). 96
Welcome to our Saviour. 142
We've been awhile a-wandering. 132
What a goodly thing. 144
What shall I give to the Child 134
What wondrous love is this. 58
When Joseph was an old man. 38
While shepherds watch'd their flocks . . . 55
Ye nations all, on you I call 86

NANCY LANGSTAFF, currently associate professor in the Creative Arts in Learning Program at Lesley College Graduate School, Cambridge, Massachusetts, has had a lifelong involvement in teaching and music. She has collaborated with John Langstaff in both performances and publications, and is the author of two books on arts in education.

JOHN LANGSTAFF has been interested in Christmas and ritual music, drama and dance all his life. His career as concert singer, recording artist, authority in the field of ritual music, author of music books, and teacher, combined with this interest, led to his founding and direction of the *Christmas Revels* —a celebratory form of participatory theater.

COLOPHON

The Christmas Revels Songbook was designed and edited at the Philidor Press in Boston by M. Sue Ladr, Scott-Martin Kosofsky, and Tom Pixton. The text was set in Scotch, a face which was first cut in 1833 at the Wilson foundry in Glasgow. Appearing in dozens, perhaps hundreds, of versions, it was the most ubiquitous of type families in 19th-century England and America. The music was set by A-R Editions of Madison, Wisconsin, using their newly developed, computerized system which can accommodate both musical notation and lyrics. The cover and title page types — Bradley, Caxton, and Atlanta — were set in original 19th-century metal from the T. J. Lyons Collection, Boston. The headband ornaments were set from a series of flowers designed by Bruce Rogers for the Monotype Corporation. The cover picture, a detail from the "Banquetting Hall, Haddon Hall, Derbyshire," is from a series of two-color lithographs by Joseph Nash, *The Mansions of England in the Olden Time* published between 1839 and 1849. It was colored for the present publication by Susan Donath. This edition was printed by the Rae Publishing Company and bound by A. Horowitz & Sons.